THE
DYNAMIC LANDSCAPE

M.J. Readman
Deputy Headmaster, Westwood High School, Leek

F.M. Mayers
Deputy Headmaster, King Edward VI School, Lichfield

Oliver & Boyd

Acknowledgements

The publishers would like to thank the following for permission to reproduce photographs:

Space Frontiers (1.1, 10.1b, 11.13, 11.16); British Petroleum Ltd (1.2a, b, 11.12); A.T. Waltham (3.5, 7.19, 9.3, 9.6a, 13.10a); Spectrum (3.6a); J. Allan Cash (13.14); F.M. Mayers (3.8, 5.1b, c, 8.8, 8.11, 12.16h, 17.1, 17.4a, c, 20.10); Barnaby's Picture Library (3.10, 6.2, 7.1, 7.2, 9.5, 10.1a, 13.8); National Coal Board (3.15); Landform Slides (3.17, 5.1d, 7.9, 7.21, 8.4, 12.16b, g, 16.1); Westfälisches Amt für Denkmalpflege (4.1a, b); Colorific (4.8 Maurice & Sally Landre, 12.9a Brian Boyd, 13.10b Claus C. Meyer, 14.6 Carl Purcell, 19.1 Earl Young, 19.6 Jim Howard, 19.7 David Burnett/Contact Press, 19.9b Gene E. Moore); R.R. Furness, Soil Survey of England and Wales (4.10); English China Clays plc (4.13a); Severn Trent Water Authority (4.13b); John and Penny Hubley (4.13c); Lennart Henrikson, Swedish National Board of Fisheries (4.15); M.J. Readman (5.1a, 17.4b); John Topham Picture Library (5.1e, 12.16e, 13.5); Keith Hollins (7.11); Camerapix-Hutchison (7.13); John Rhodes (7.16, 14.1a, b); J. Francis (8.12); G.S. Pringle (9.1); Aerophoto Eelde (9.6b); R.W. Mason (11.4b); P.P. Hattinga Verschure (11.9b); Rex Features (11.10); Brian Lee (12.10); Mary Evans Picture Library (12.11); E.W. Smith (12.16a); Bruce Coleman (12.16c, 20.1a); Jon Martin (12.16d, f); Geoslides (13.9, 20.1b); John Player, RTZ Oil and Gas (13.10c); Zambia National Tourist Board (14.7); Oxfam (15.7); Douglas Dickins (15.8); J.B. Thornes (16.6); Tony Morrison (16.7); Picturepoint (19.9a); Bryan and Cherry Alexander (20.7a, b);

The title page photograph is by J. Allan Cash and shows landslip effects of erosion at Warden Point, Isle of Sheppey, Kent.

Illustrations on page 48 by Bob Geary; illustration 19.1a on page 84 by Don Harley

Oliver & Boyd
Robert Stevenson House
1–3 Baxter's Place
Leith Walk
Edinburgh EH1 3BB
A division of Longman Group Ltd

ISBN 0 05 003806 0
First published 1986

Produced by Longman Group (FE) Ltd
Printed in Hong Kong

Contents

Discovering

For most of the time that people have been on earth they have only been able to see as far as the horizon, and have always been curious to see what lay beyond it. Aeroplanes gave us a better view of our earth but it was not until the late 1960s that satellites allowed us to view our planet from space (1.1 shows a satellite picture of Britain). Despite this great step forward, there are still very many unanswered questions about our earth.

▼ **1.2a** Calbeck Ness before the oil terminal was built

1.1 Britain from space ▶

There are two groups of factors at work in shaping the landscape of any part of the earth's surface: *physical* and *human* factors. Physical factors such as **rock type** and **climate** were at work long before the human race evolved. Now, human and physical factors act together. In order to survive, people have often had to change the environment. But, if the beauty and resources of the earth are not to be destroyed, we must gain a deep understanding of the natural world.

Both physical and human factors can change with time. Some changes are so slow that they are not noticed in a person's lifetime. Others, such as an earthquake or a volcanic explosion, can change the shape of the land in a matter of seconds. Human activity brings about many changes to the landscape. 1.2a and b show how the discovery of offshore oil has completely changed the appearance of Calbeck Ness in Shetland. Sullom Voe oil terminal (the largest in Europe) was built on this land.

◀ **1.2b** Calbeck Ness after the oil terminal was built

A scientific approach

Whether the landscape is dominated by physical or human factors, or is a mixture of both, it can only be fully understood if a logical scientific approach is used (1.3). An important part of this is to decide beforehand what the aim of the study is and to concentrate only on information (data) relevant to this. To describe everything in sight (although better than nothing) is much less likely to give worthwhile results.

Any landscape is complex and it is important to have a checklist of factors which might be at work. Some of these will be working today and some will have been important in the past. 1.4 summarises the possible human and physical *inputs*, past and present, to any landscape. Look again at 1.2 and see how many of the inputs you can identify. It is interesting to note that the Sullom Voe oil terminal may be a temporary landscape feature as the offshore oil supplies nearby are likely to be used up before very long.

▼ **1.3** Steps in studying a landscape

1. Decide what is the aim of the landscape study	2. Decide how to organise the study	3. Collect data relevent to aim	4. Organise and display data	5. Analyse data collected	6. Draw conclusions about landscape

◄ **1.4** Inputs to a landscape

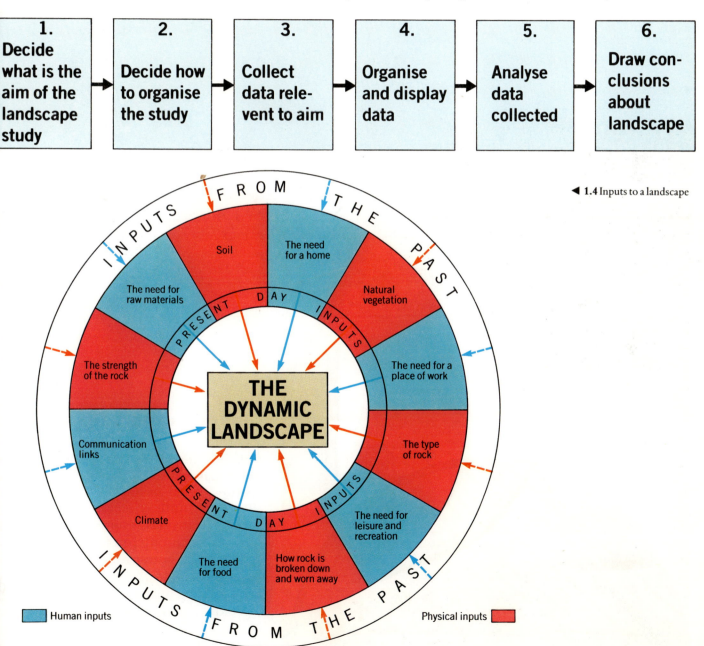

INPUTS FROM THE PAST

Soil · The need for a home · The need for raw materials · Natural vegetation · The strength of the rock · The need for a place of work · Communication links · The type of rock · Climate · The need for leisure and recreation · The need for food · How rock is broken down and worn away

PRESENT DAY INPUTS

THE DYNAMIC LANDSCAPE

INPUTS FROM THE PAST

■ Human inputs   Physical inputs ■

5

2   The active earth

Death and destruction

At any moment, somewhere in the world, an earthquake may strike or a volcano erupt. The result may be the destruction of many lives, buildings or forests. Powerful forces like these have been around for millions of years. 2.1 is a newspaper account of a small earthquake that happened in Britain in 1896.

Even today, although geologists understand a great deal about the causes of earthquakes and volcanoes, it is still very difficult to predict exactly when or where they will strike. What we do know is that they tend to occur most often in certain parts of the world. These 'zones of activity' can be plotted on a map, as shown on 2.2.

▼ **2.1** The Hereford earthquake

▼ **2.2** Distribution of earthquakes and volcanoes

Area where earthquakes and volcanoes are most likely

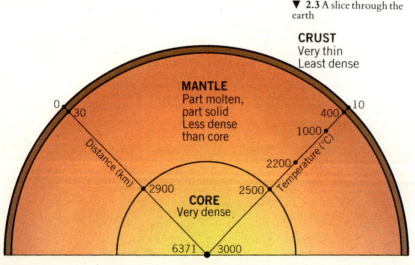

Hereford Mercury.
December 17th, 1896
THE EARTHQUAKE
SEVERE SHOCKS AT HEREFORD THIS MORNING.
WIDESPREAD DISTURBANCE.
SERIOUS DAMAGE TO PROPERTY.
CATHEDRAL TOWER AFFECTED.
MANY NARROW ESCAPES.
UNIVERSAL CONSTERNATION.
SPECIAL INQUIRIES BY OUR REPRESENTATIVES
TELEGRAMS FROM CORRESPONDENTS.

▼ **2.3** A slice through the earth

CRUST
Very thin
Least dense

MANTLE
Part molten,
part solid
Less dense
than core

Distance (km)

Temperature (°C)

0   30   400   10
1000
2200
2900   2500
CORE
Very dense
6371   3000

Inside the earth

Earthquakes and volcanoes tell us a great deal about the inside of the earth. The earth has been cooling down over the 4000 million years since it was formed. This has resulted in the formation of a thin outer **crust** which lies on top of much hotter rocks. The crust can be compared to the skin that forms on top of a mug of hot milk when it cools.

Below the crust there are other layers of rock. These get hotter and hotter towards the centre of the earth where the rock may be solid or liquid (see 2.3).

There are two main types of crust. **Oceanic crust** (mostly made of basalt) forms a layer round the earth and is found under the oceans and under the continents. The top layer of the continents is another type of crust called **continental crust** which is mostly made of granite. This is less dense than basalt, so it floats on top, as you can see in 2.4.

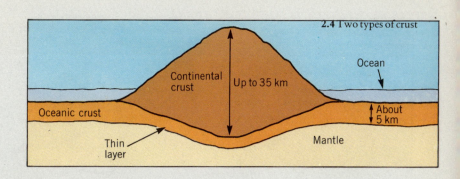

2.4 Two types of crust

Moving continents

The earth's crust is not made of one continuous sheet of rock. It is divided into sections or **plates**. These fit together like the pieces of a jigsaw but with straighter edges. The plates are moving towards or away from each other at the rate of a few millimetres a year. Over millions of years great distances can be covered.

It is believed that the plates move because of **convection currents** moving from the hot inner parts of the earth. These currents are rather like the ones in a pan of boiling rice (see 2.5). As the plates move, so do the continents that sit on top of them. 2.6 shows how the shapes and positions of the continents

◀ **2.5** Convection currents in a pan of rice

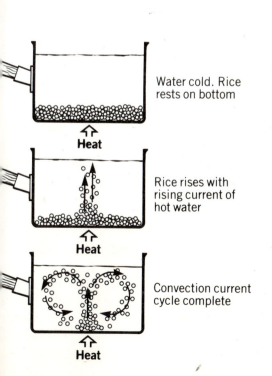

Water cold. Rice rests on bottom

Heat

Rice rises with rising current of hot water

Heat

Convection current cycle complete

Heat

▶ **2.6** The drifting continents

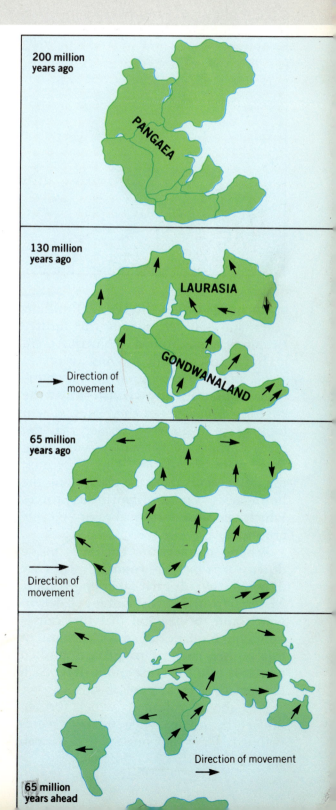

200 million years ago

PANGAEA

130 million years ago

LAURASIA

GONDWANALAND

→ Direction of movement

65 million years ago

→ Direction of movement

65 million years ahead

Direction of movement →

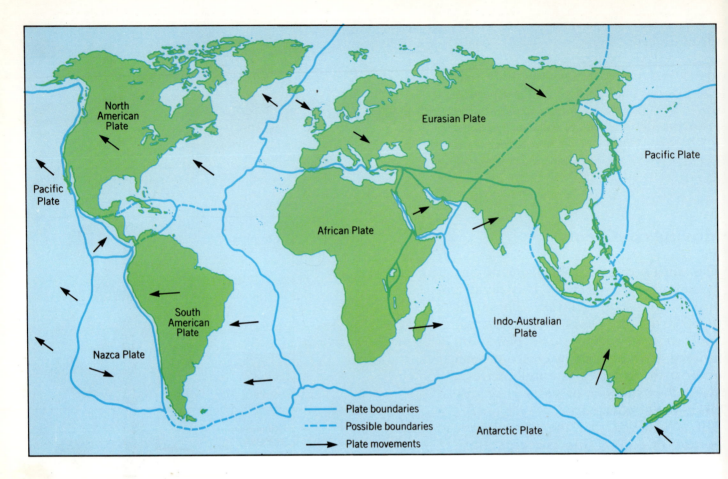

have changed over the last 200 million years and will change in the future. Britain was once joined to North America but is now steadily moving away.

2.7 shows the position of the continents as they are now. It also shows the edges or *boundaries* of the plates. If you look back at 2.2 you can see that the earth's 'zones of activity' occur along these plate boundaries. This is because the movements that take place along the boundaries set up enormous forces which can cause earthquakes or volcanic eruptions.

Where convection currents move downwards into the **mantle**, plates are dragged towards each other and collide. Material from the crust is dragged downwards and the friction that this causes melts huge quantities of rock. Some of this molten rock or **magma** is pushed upwards into the crust and it may reach the surface to form a volcano.

2.8a shows volcanoes which formed under the ocean when oceanic plates collided. They stick out above the ocean surface as islands and often form lines of volcanic islands called **island arcs**. 2.8b shows what happens when two continental plates collide. Some volcanoes occur. Also, the rocks from the ocean which was between the two continents are squashed together and lifted up to form **fold mountains**. 2.8c shows what happens when oceanic and continental plates collide.

Where convection currents move upwards, plates are pushed apart and material from the mantle is moved up to form new crust. When this happens under the oceans, it results in large **mountain ridges** with a trench in between them (see 2.8e). Some of the world's largest mountains are hidden under the sea in **ocean ridges**. When the currents move upwards under continental crust, **rift valleys** are formed as the plates move apart, and volcanoes occur in and around them (2.8d). These valleys often have steep sides and may contain lakes or rivers.

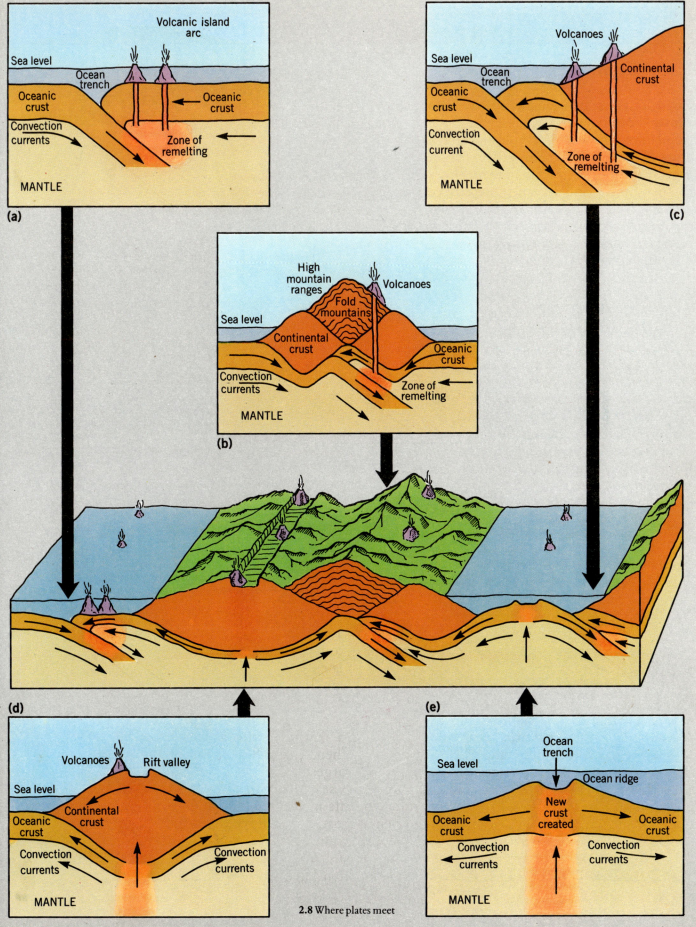

(a) Volcanic island arc — Sea level — Ocean trench — Oceanic crust — Oceanic crust — Convection currents — Zone of remelting — MANTLE

(c) Volcanoes — Sea level — Ocean trench — Continental crust — Oceanic crust — Convection current — Zone of remelting — MANTLE

(b) High mountain ranges — Volcanoes — Fold mountains — Sea level — Continental crust — Oceanic crust — Convection currents — Zone of remelting — MANTLE

(d) Volcanoes — Rift valley — Sea level — Continental crust — Oceanic crust — Convection currents — Convection currents — MANTLE

(e) Ocean trench — Sea level — Ocean ridge — New crust created — Oceanic crust — Oceanic crust — Convection currents — Convection currents — MANTLE

2.8 Where plates meet

Volcanic power

Guadeloupe is an island which is on a **plate** boundary. 3.1 describes the tremendous power of a volcano which erupted there in 1976. This power brings great quantities of gas and new materials to the surface and is called **extrusive** activity. When **magma** is moved into the crust, but does not reach the surface (until the rocks on top are worn away), it is called **intrusive** activity.

Volcanoes vary in shape and size depending on whether they are made from **ash** (pieces of shattered rock thrown from the crater), one of several different types of **lava**, or a mixture of both. Gases and steam also play a part in eruptions, but have few long-term effects. 3.2 shows a **composite cone**, the most usual type, where ash and lava make up alternate layers. If the main **vent** is blocked, **secondary cones** may form where magma is forced to the surface by another route.

▼ **3.1** *Evening Standard*, 16 August 1976

'VOLCANO OF ATOM BOMBS'

POINTE-A-PITRE
Guadaloupe, Monday
THOUSANDS of panic-stricken people have fled from the shadow of Guadeloupe's belching volcano La Soufriere, which experts say could explode at any moment with a force of perhaps 17 times that of the atom bomb dropped on Hiroshima.

An estimated 130,000 people clogged narrow roads with buses, cars, handcarts, and horse-drawn carriages as they tried to escape from the capital of Basse-Terre, western of the twin islands which form the French West Indian department.

They made for the far side of Basse-Terre, to relatives' homes and to hastily-prepared refugee camps.

As hot ash rained down on villages around the 4868-foot volcano, Basse-Terre Prefect Jean Aurosseau said: "We consider that we are entering a phase that can only end in a giant eruption... the countdown has begun."

The evacuation was ordered after French scientists studied the volcano, which has been active since July 8 when an eruption ripped one of its flanks.

French volcano expert Pierre Brousse, interviewed on the neighbouring island of Dominica, said the eruption would begin within 12 hours.

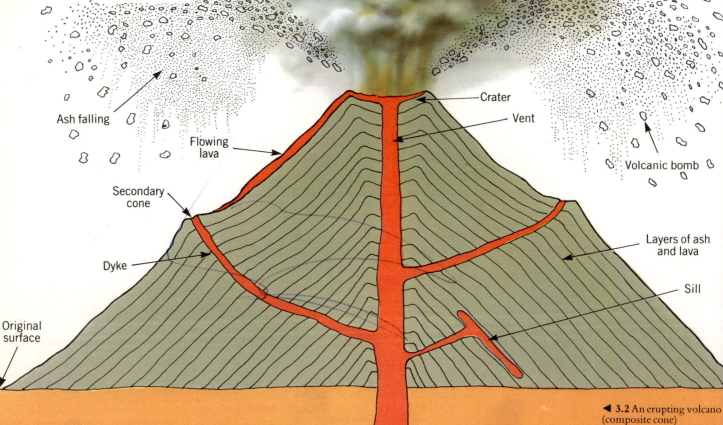

Steam, gas and dust

Ash falling

Flowing lava

Secondary cone

Dyke

Original surface

Crater

Vent

Volcanic bomb

Layers of ash and lava

Sill

◄ **3.2** An erupting volcano (composite cone)

Magma chamber

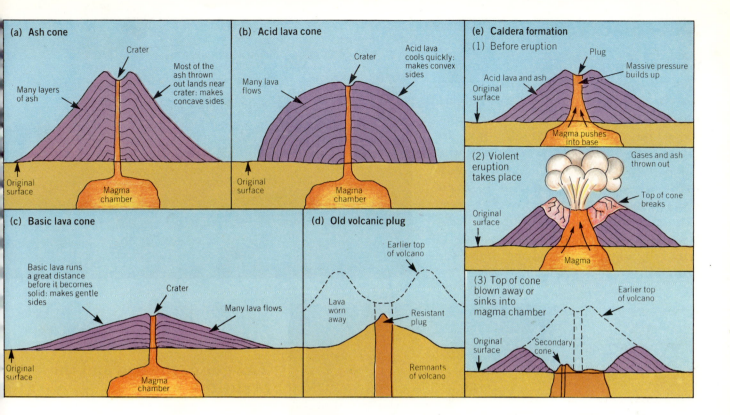

(a) Ash cone
Crater
Many layers of ash
Most of the ash thrown out lands near crater: makes concave sides
Original surface
Magma chamber

(b) Acid lava cone
Crater
Many lava flows
Acid lava cools quickly: makes convex sides
Original surface
Magma chamber

(c) Basic lava cone
Basic lava runs a great distance before it becomes solid: makes gentle sides
Crater
Many lava flows
Original surface
Magma chamber

(d) Old volcanic plug
Earlier top of volcano
Lava worn away
Resistant plug
Remnants of volcano

(e) Caldera formation
(1) Before eruption
Plug
Massive pressure builds up
Acid lava and ash
Original surface
Magma pushes into base

(2) Violent eruption takes place
Gases and ash thrown out
Original surface
Top of cone breaks
Magma

(3) Top of cone blown away or sinks into magma chamber
Earlier top of volcano
Original surface
Secondary cone

▲ **3.3** Other types of volcanoes

3.3a shows the concave slope of cones formed by ash alone. Monte Nuova in Italy is an example. In just three days it grew to over 150 metres high.

The shape of lava cones depends on how far the lava flows before cooling and becoming solid. The cone in 3.3b is made of **acid lava** (silica rich) which only flows a short distance before setting. Puy-de-Dôme in France is an example. It is dome shaped with convex sides.

3.3c shows a cone made of **basic lava** (low in silica), which flows great distances before setting. It therefore has very gentle sloping sides. Mauna Loa in Hawaii is an example. It stands about 10 km above the sea floor, but slopes at such a gentle angle that it is about 480 km in diameter.

Once activity stops, magma in the crater and vent solidifies, forming a cap of solid rock above molten material, like a plug in a bottle. 3.3d shows how this **plug** may, after many years, be left as a steep-sided column of rock. However, plugs may prevent magma from passing up the vent. Massive pressure then builds up, swelling the volcano's base.

This may eventually cause the type of violent eruption shown in 3.3e where the top of the volcano is completely removed. Crater Lake in Oregon was formed when water filled the enormous **caldera** (crater) left after the top 2000 metres of the volcano blew off. The lake is now almost 10 km wide.

Not all eruptions are violent. Large areas of the world are covered by basic lava flows which gently spread out from cracks (fissures). 3.4 shows how a series of flows can cover all the original surface. The different layers of lava are clearly seen in northern Iceland where rivers have cut through the flows.

▼ **3.4** A river cutting through lava flows

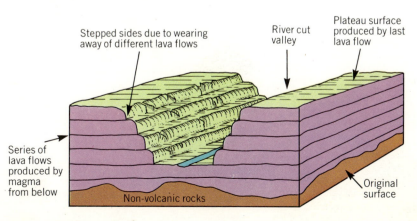

Stepped sides due to wearing away of different lava flows
River cut valley
Plateau surface produced by last lava flow
Series of lava flows produced by magma from below
Non-volcanic rocks
Original surface

11

Never trust a volcano

Extinct (dead) volcanoes show no signs of activity and are usually fairly ancient. We do not expect them to erupt again. **Dormant** (sleeping) volcanoes also show no signs of activity, but are thought to have erupted fairly recently. They may erupt again. **Active** volcanoes are definitely known to have erupted in recent times. However, even extinct volcanoes may not be safe. Vesuvius was thought to be extinct in A.D. 79, when it erupted and destroyed Pompeii.

▲ **3.5** Terraced volcanic slopes

► **3.6a** A geyser in Iceland

The good, the bad and the beautiful

Although volcanoes can be very destructive, many people choose to live near them. This may seem surprising, but there are often good reasons for doing so. For example, rich soils form on the volcanic **deposits**, which are excellent for farming. 3.5 shows how in Bali in Indonesia the inhabitants terrace the steep slopes to make full use of the land. In some parts of the world, valuable materials such as gold, iron and diamonds have been formed by volcanic activity, and large mining centres have developed.

In Iceland, volcanic rocks near the surface are so hot that water found near them can be used for heating homes and greenhouses, or for making steam to generate electricity. It is likely that, by pumping water deep underground in parts of Britain, to where hot rocks lie, Britain could also benefit from this cheap and pollution-free energy source.

Volcanic areas are often spectacularly beautiful and may attract tourists. **Geysers** such as those shown in 3.6a are particularly popular. 3.6b explains how they are formed by water and steam being forced out of a narrow opening under great pressure.

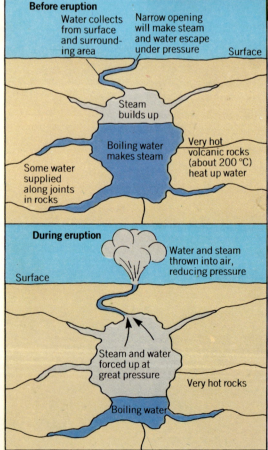

Before eruption
Water collects from surface and surrounding area
Narrow opening will make steam and water escape under pressure
Surface
Steam builds up
Boiling water makes steam
Very hot volcanic rocks (about 200 °C) heat up water
Some water supplied along joints in rocks

During eruption
Surface
Water and steam thrown into air, reducing pressure
Steam and water forced up at great pressure
Very hot rocks
Boiling water

◄ **3.6b** The formation of geysers

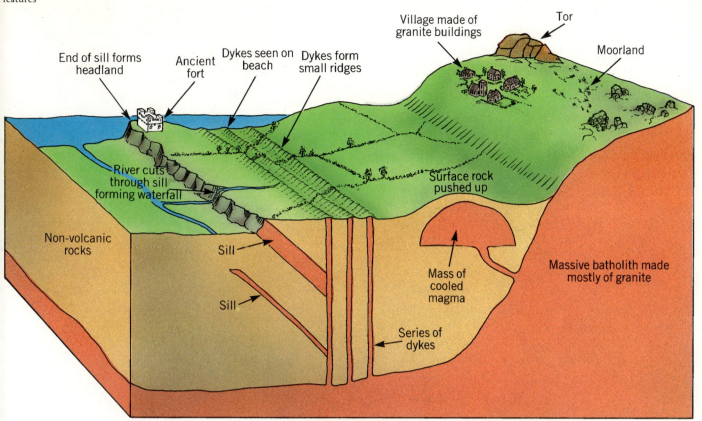

End of sill forms headland

Ancient fort

Dykes seen on beach

Dykes form small ridges

Village made of granite buildings

Tor

Moorland

River cuts through sill forming waterfall

Non-volcanic rocks

Sill

Sill

Surface rock pushed up

Mass of cooled magma

Series of dykes

Massive batholith made mostly of granite

Late to the surface

Intrusive activity can be important in shaping the land. 3.7 displays the major ways in which this happens. Granite **batholiths** form when huge quantities of magma move into the crust, often under mountain ranges. If the rocks above are removed, bleak moorlands are formed topped by **tors**. 3.8 shows how these tors appear as blocks of rock steadily worn down by the weather.

Different-shaped masses of magma may break away from the batholith, pushing up the surface rocks in places.

Magma may be forced like a massive sheet between layers of non-volcanic rocks to form **sills**. If sheets of magma cross these layers or rocks, **dykes** are formed. When sills and dykes are exposed they are normally harder than local rocks and worn down more slowly, forming ridges. If they are softer than local rocks they form depressions or ditches.

3.9 lists the most important effects of volcanoes on people.

◀ **3.8** Tors

▼ **3.9** The effects of volcanoes

Positive effects	Negative effects
1. Some **weathered** lava makes fertile soil and rich farming land.	1. Can cause loss of life, especially from being buried by ash or release of gases.
2. Sometimes precious minerals such as diamonds, or useful materials such as copper, nickel or sulphur are formed.	2. Can cause *tsunami* (huge sea waves) and even greater loss of life. (See page 15.)
3. Hot springs may be used for heating or to supply hot water.	3. Can cause great damage to property or farmland, if lava or ash covers the area.
4. Hot volcanic rocks may be used to make **geothermal power**.	4. Can lead to short-term changes in the climate, where volcanic dust in the atmosphere blocks out some of the sun's heat.
5. Some volcanic areas may attract tourists, helping the economy of the area.	

Suddenly the ground explodes

'I heard a noise as if a whole squadron of jets was approaching. It got louder and louder and then it went "boom" like a bomb. There was a colossal thrust upwards, then from side to side.' This eye witness of the Italian earthquake of 1980 was lucky. Over 1000 people out of 3000 in his town, shown in 3.10, were killed by the quake which lasted just 90 seconds.

Earthquakes occur when sudden movements take place within and below the crust. Shock waves are sent out, and

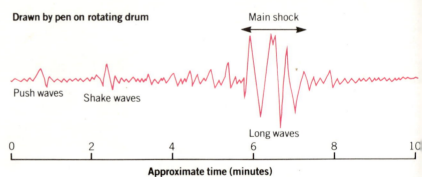

Drawn by pen on rotating drum

Main shock

Push waves   Shake waves

Long waves

0   2   4   6   8   10

Approximate time (minutes)

▲ **3.11a** Seismic trace

▼ **3.11b** The intensity scale of earthquakes

2	Hardly felt.
4	Hanging objects swing. Windows, dishes and doors rattle. Heavy vibration.
6	Felt by all. Many people frightened and run outdoors. Difficult to walk. Windows broken and furniture overturned.
8	Some buildings collapse. Cracks open in ground. Some tall chimneys fall. Branches break off trees.
10	Most buildings destroyed. Large landslides. Serious damage to dams and bridges. Underground pipes broken and rail lines bend.
12	Damage nearly total. Objects thrown into the air. Large areas of ground moved up or down.

it is these which cause damage. The **seismic trace** in 3.11a shows the usual pattern of earthquakes. **Push waves** travelling in straight lines from the **focus** reach the surface first, while the shaking motion of **shake waves** slows their progress. **Long waves** are formed when push and shake waves reach the surface and travel along it. They arrive last but are the most destructive.

The intensity of earthquakes is usually measured on the Mercalli scale, using different things felt or noticed by people. Parts of this scale are set out in 3.11b.

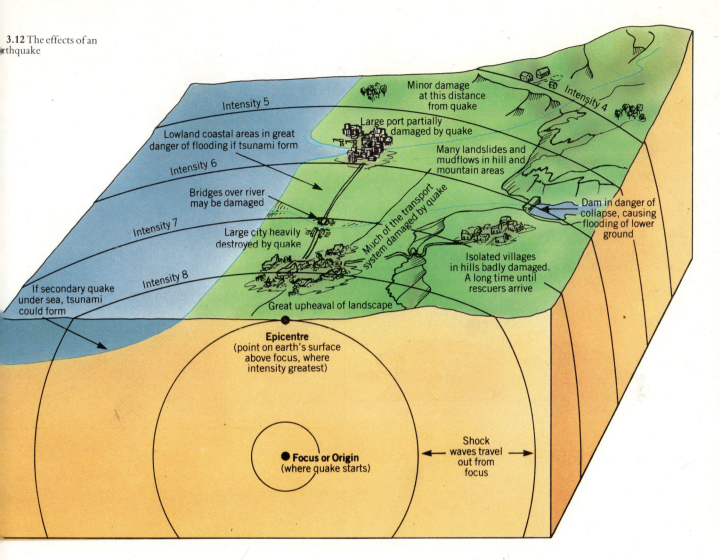

Intensity 5

Minor damage at this distance from quake

Intensity 4

Lowland coastal areas in great danger of flooding if tsunami form

Large port partially damaged by quake

Intensity 6

Many landslides and mudflows in hill and mountain areas

Bridges over river may be damaged

Dam in danger of collapse, causing flooding of lower ground

Intensity 7

Large city heavily destroyed by quake

Much of the transport system damaged by quake

Intensity 8

Isolated villages in hills badly damaged. A long time until rescuers arrive

If secondary quake under sea, tsunami could form

Great upheaval of landscape

Epicentre
(point on earth's surface above focus, where intensity greatest)

● **Focus or Origin**
(where quake starts)

Shock waves travel out from focus

The point where the earth movement takes place is called the origin or focus. Shock waves are felt first and most strongly at the **epicentre**, the point on the surface above the focus. Moving away from the epicentre the damage done lessens. 3.12 shows the different ways in which earthquakes can affect an area 3.13 lists some major quakes and describes the damage caused by the Kanto quake in Japan.

Tsunami (huge sea waves) are particularly feared. Quakes under the sea can lift the seabed, forming giant waves travelling at up to 700 km/h, swamping lowland areas. In 1896 a tsunami off Japan killed 27 000 people.

Date	Epicentre	Magnitude	Deaths
1906	San Francisco	8.3	700
1923	Kanto (Japan)	8.3	142 807
1940	E. Turkey	7.9	40 000
1948	Fukui (Japan)	7.3	5 386
1976	Turkey	7.9	5 000

Damage caused by 1923 earthquake, Kanto

To people			To houses
Deaths	99 331	Totally collapsed	128 266
Injured	103 733	Half collapsed	126 233
Missing	43 476	Destroyed by fire	447 094
		Washed away by flood	868

▲ **3.13** Some major earthquakes

▼ 3.14 Folding

(a) Folds

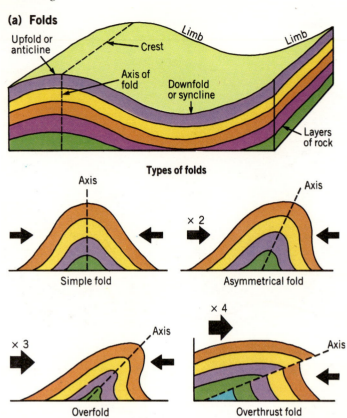

Types of folds

Simple fold
Asymmetrical fold
Overfold
Overthrust fold

(b) The formation of fold mountains

1. Two plates move steadily closer. Sediments from continents deposited into the sea between them. Deep deposits build up and sea bed sinks under this great weight.

2. As plates move nearer, sediments are squashed forming islands in the sea.

3. Sediments squashed, folded and lifted up to form fold mountains.

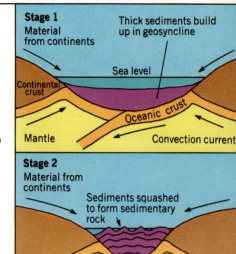

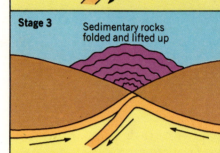

Pushing and folding

As movements take place in the crust, layers of rocks may be folded in a variety of ways shown in 3.14a. A simple fold produces a symmetrical pattern, with an upfold or **anticline**, and downfold or **syncline**. The centre line of each fold is called the axis, and the two sides are limbs. Folds where one side is steeper than the other are called asymmetrical. Here the forces on each side compressing (squashing) the rocks are not equal. A much greater force on one side could cause an **overfold**. If the compression is great enough, the rocks along the axis may break, causing an **overthrust fold**. 3.15 is a typical fold that can often be seen where rocks are exposed.

3.14b shows the way in which the movement of two plates can compress huge quantities of rocks to form **fold mountains**. All the major mountain ranges of the world were formed in this way.

▼ 3.15 Folding

16

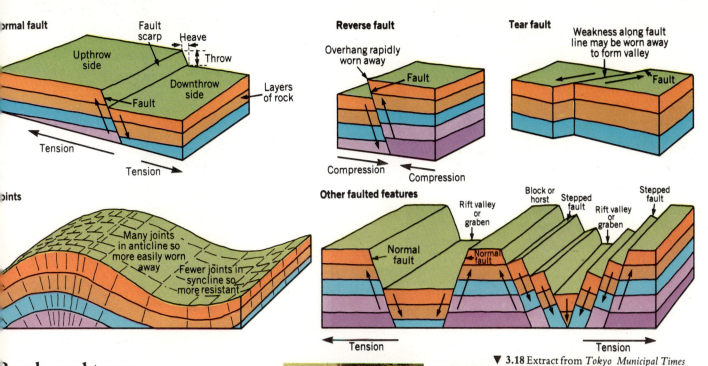

Normal fault

Fault scarp

Heave

Throw

Upthrow side

Downthrow side

Fault

Layers of rock

Tension

Tension

Reverse fault

Overhang rapidly worn away

Fault

Compression

Compression

Tear fault

Weakness along fault line may be worn away to form valley

Fault

Joints

Many joints in anticline so more easily worn away

Fewer joints in syncline so more resistant

Other faulted features

Block or horst

Stepped fault

Stepped fault

Rift valley or graben

Rift valley or graben

Normal fault

Normal fault

Tension

Tension

Breaks and tears

Where part of the crust moves along lines of weakness, rocks may fracture (break) and **faults** form. The most usual types are illustrated in 3.16. **Normal faults** (such as that shown in 3.17) are due to tension set up by parts of the crust moving apart. **Reverse faults** are the result of compression as parts of the crust move together. **Tear faults** result from sections of the crust moving across the surface in different directions. **Rift valleys** are caused by the slipping down of a section of land between two faults.

Folding and faulting may compress or expand rocks, making them less or more easy to wear away. For example, 3.16 shows how folding may cause many more **joints** in an anticline than a syncline, making it much more easily worn down.

Little can be done to prevent earthquakes, but some cities, such as Tokyo, do at least advise their inhabitants on what to do (3.18). 3.19 summarises the types of damage earthquakes cause, and suggests ways in which it could be reduced. It also outlines the reasons why poor countries are often more badly affected than rich ones.

▲ 3.17 A normal fault

▼ 3.19 Earthquake damage

▼ **3.18** Extract from *Tokyo Municipal Times*

Tokyo Metropolitan Government

What to do if a big earthquake hits

The worst shake is over in about a minute, so keep calm and quickly do the following:

1. Turn off all stoves and heaters. Put out fires that may break out. Do not become flustered by the sight of flames, and act quickly to put out the fire.
2. Get under a table or desk to protect yourself.
3. Do not run outdoors where you are liable to be hit by falling objects.
4. Open the door for an emergency exit. Door frames are liable to spring in a big quake and hold the doors so tight they cannot be opened.
5. Keep away from narrow alleys, concrete block walls, embankments and take temporary refuge in an open area.
6. For evacuation from department stores or theaters, do not panic and do as directed by the attendant in charge.
7. When driving in the streets, move the car to the left and stop. Driving will be banned in restricted areas.
8. Evacuate to a designated safety evacuation area when a big fire or other danger approaches.
9. Walk to emergency evacuation areas. Take the minimum of personal belongings.
10. Do not be moved by rumors. Listen for the latest news over the radio.

Main types of earthquake damage

1. Parts of crust move because of faults or fractures.
2. Part of seabed raised or lowered causing tsunami.
3. Landslides and mudslides, especially in hilly areas.
4. Settlements destroyed, buildings collapse or flooded. Fires start and water becomes polluted causing disease.

How poor countries miss out

1. Less money to spend on research. Warnings of earthquakes and tsunami less reliable.
2. Less money to spend on planning for earthquakes.
3. Fewer hospitals, doctors and drugs.
4. Roads, railways and telephone services often poor: help takes much longer to arrive.
5. Less money to spend on rebuilding after the quake.

How to prevent damage to property and life

1. Avoid high-rise buildings: single storey where possible.
2. Buildings should have strengthened foundations and be able to stand up to rocking movements of quakes.
3. Use lightweight building materials.
4. Gas, water, sewage and electric supplies should be carried in flexible pipes.
5. Emergency shelters should be provided above flood levels and away from fire dangers.
6. Regular earthquake drills should take place.
7. Families should have their own emergency supplies of food, drugs, water, blankets, etc.
8. Emergency centres should have stocks of food, drugs, etc., to be sent out rapidly when needed.

Types of weathering

Most rocks are gradually softened or broken down by wind, rain and sun. This process is called **weathering**. It often causes costly damage to roads and buildings.

The type of weathering which takes place, and the speed at which it takes place, depends on a number of factors. The make up of the **rock**, the **climate**, the **soil** and the **vegetation** are all important. Also, if there is air pollution, the gases in the air may react with rainwater to form chemicals which are capable of rotting the rock. Photographs 4.1a and b show how this has happened to a sandstone statue in an industrial town.

Breaking up

If an empty ring-pull can is pressed in and out a few times the metal will split because of metal fatigue. **Mechanical weathering** of rocks is similar. Rock breaks when it has been put under repeated stress and strain. 4.2a shows what can happen when the surface of bare rock is heated and cooled many times. This is best seen in hot deserts such as the Sahara, where rock expands in the heat of the day but contracts at night when the lack of cloud lets temperatures fall rapidly. There is little vegetation or soil to protect the rock from these extremes of temperature. This is sometimes called **onion weathering** because the surface layers split off like the layers of an onion.

In 4.2b **freeze–thaw** is shown. If a rock **outcrop** has lots of cracks in it, water may enter and freeze at night. In time, bits of rock break off because water expands by about 8% when it forms ice and this puts strain on the rock. (This is why water pipes may burst if allowed to freeze in winter.)

(a)

(b)

◀ **4.1** A statue in the Ruhr industrial area before and after acidification

Freeze–thaw is most important where the temperature rises above and falls below 0 °C many times during the year. Sharp angular bits of rock at the bottom of a slope are usually a sign that mechanical weathering has been taking place.

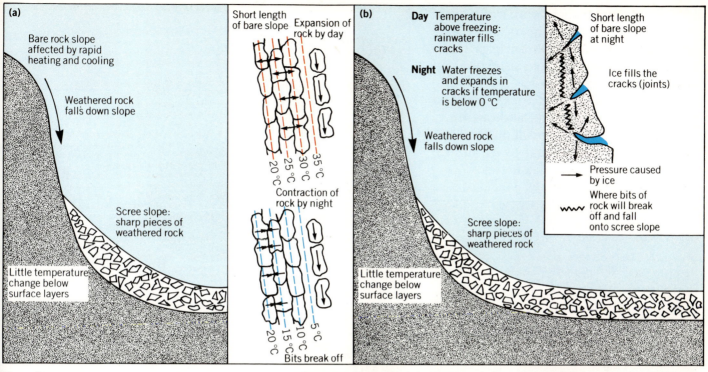

▼ **4.2a** Rock fatigue caused by heating and cooling

(a)

Bare rock slope affected by rapid heating and cooling

Weathered rock falls down slope

Scree slope: sharp pieces of weathered rock

Little temperature change below surface layers

Short length of bare slope

Expansion of rock by day

35 °C 30 °C 25 °C 20 °C

Contraction of rock by night

5 °C 10 °C 15 °C 20 °C

Bits break off

▼ **4.2b** Rock fatigue caused by freezing and thawing

(b)

Day Temperature above freezing: rainwater fills cracks

Night Water freezes and expands in cracks if temperature is below 0 °C

Weathered rock falls down slope

Scree slope: sharp pieces of weathered rock

Little temperature change below surface layers

Short length of bare slope at night

Ice fills the cracks (joints)

→ Pressure caused by ice

〰 Where bits of rock will break off and fall onto scree slope

Rock eaters

The main types of **chemical weathering** are shown in 4.3. Water is needed for all the changes to take place. It may come either from rain or from dampness in the air. Even in hot deserts the air contains tiny amounts of moisture which can chemically change rock. Rocks are made up of one or more substances called minerals and it is these which are changed. Most minerals break down to form tiny clay-sized particles. But quartz (or sand), which is the most common mineral, is left unchanged.

Chemical weathering takes place most rapidly in hot and wet areas of the world. 4.4 shows how weathering increases with temperature. Where certain types of air pollution are found, building stone will rot very quickly. The sandstone statue in 4.1 is from the Ruhr industrial area of Germany where gases such as sulphur dioxide are in the air. When mixed with rain, these form sulphuric acid which rots the stone. More information on chemical weathering can be found on pages 22 and 23.

4.3 Types of chemical weathering

Weathering caused by increase in size of rock minerals

1. **Oxidation**. Oxygen from the air is added to metals in rocks to form oxides.

2. **Hydration**. Water is added to minerals in rocks, making them larger. In both cases the rock crumbles.

Weathering caused by major chemical change in minerals

1. **Hydrolysis**. Water reacts with minerals and breaks them down.

2. **Carbonation and solution**. Water reacts with carbonate minerals to make them soluble.

4.4 Chemical weathering and temperature

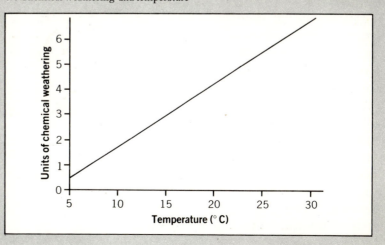

Plant power

Plants and animals help both mechanical and chemical weathering to take place, as 4.5 shows. Activities such as quarrying and forest clearance also speed up weathering.

The breakdown of rocks gives a foothold for plant roots and, in time, soil will form. Without soil no food can be grown, so soil is vital to us all. 4.6 shows what a fertile soil contains.

Increase mechanical weathering

1. **Plant roots** force open cracks in the rock as roots grow deeper and wider.

2. **Swaying trees** widen cracks and weaken rock as trees sway in wind and roots move.

Increase chemical weathering

1. **Burrowing animals** let air and water through soil to weather rock.

2. **Rotting plant remains** make humic acids which mix with water and then react with minerals in rocks.

▲ **4.5** Types of biological weathering

Soil

▶ **4.7** Model soil profile for Britain

A fertile soil needs the correct balance of ingredients. If too much sand is present the soil will be dry. Too much clay will make the soil wet and hard to cultivate. 4.7 shows what happens in Britain when soil forms over a long period of time. A slice taken downwards (**a soil profile**) shows layering. Colour and texture differences allow separate bands to be identified (labelled A, B, C). Each band can be subdivided (A_0, A_1, etc.) if necessary. In wet climates water often washes plant food (minerals) downwards. This is called **leaching**. In dry climates heat draws water and minerals upwards. Fertile soils do not show much water movement in either direction.

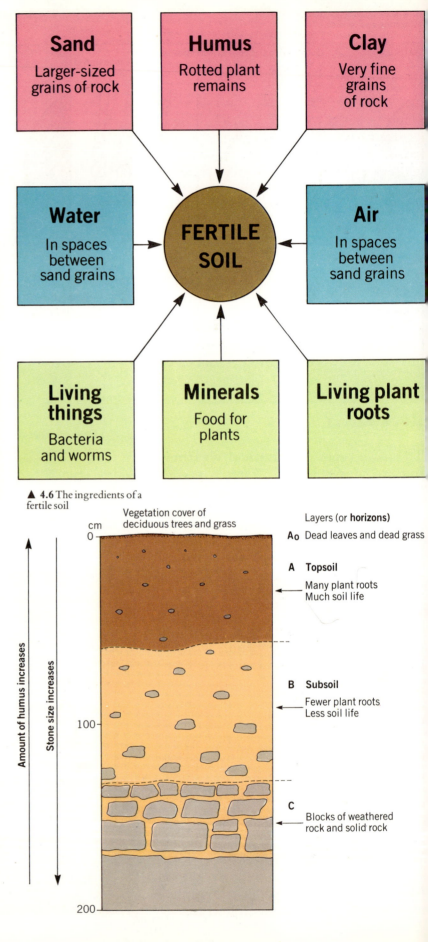

▲ **4.6** The ingredients of a fertile soil

The amount of food that can be grown depends partly on the type and quality of soil. Loss of soil by **erosion** is very serious as 4.8 shows.

In the background of the photograph the vegetation can be seen with its roots in the darker **topsoil**. The dark colour is due to **humus**. In the foreground all the topsoil has been removed leaving the yellow **subsoil**. Rainwater flowing down the slope has cut into the subsoil forming small gulleys or rills. The subsoil is infertile and any plant which gets a hold will be short of food and in danger of being washed away by the next rainstorm. None of this would have happened if the vegetation had not been cleared.

The way that soil, vegetation and climate are linked has only recently been fully understood. Vegetation has often been cleared to grow food, and the soil has been damaged. To correct this damage is costly or even impossible. Prevention of soil erosion is obviously much better.

4.9 shows how the rate of soil erosion in Britain varies as the use of the land changes. The original forest cover prevented much erosion by breaking the force of the rain with branches and by binding soil together with roots. The greatest danger was when the land was temporarily bare of protection in 1870 and 1950.

The force of wind can do as much damage as water, as 4.10 shows. In East Anglia arable fields have been made larger by digging up hedges. The hedges used to act as windbreaks. In a dry spring the wind may blow the loose most fertile topsoil away before crop roots can bind it together. Snow ploughs sometimes have to be used to clear lanes.

◄ **4.8** Soil erosion in the southern USA

▼ **4.9** Erosion rates and land use in lowland Britain

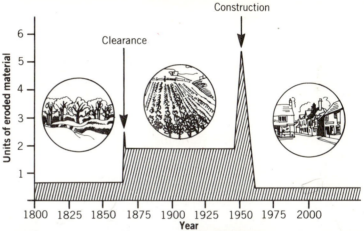

► **4.10** Wind erosion in East Anglia

In any area the soil, plants and animals all depend on each other. This is called an **ecosystem**. 4.11a shows five common ways of changing an ecosystem and so allowing water and/or wind to destroy soil fertility. Even slight erosion is serious because the small light bits of soil are the most fertile and will be carried away first. In the past, few people worried about the problem, but 4.11b shows just how serious the problem has become in the USA. With more people needing more food the US Government set up the Soil Conservation Service to try to improve badly eroded areas and prevent erosion elsewhere.

Ways of preventing soil erosion are shown in 4.12. Some, such as **contour ploughing**, involve no extra cost but others, such as **terracing**, are expensive. The methods all aim to reduce the amount of water running down slopes and to keep the amount of bare soil as small as possible. A balanced ecosystem is the aim. Poor areas of the world, which need to grow more and more food, need most help in understanding how to prevent soil erosion.

Water	Wind and water
1. **Deforestation**. Trees cleared for farming. Branches stopped the force of rain, and roots held soil together. Once land is cleared, bare soil is washed away.	1. **Overgrazing**. Too many animals kept: they eat all grass leaves. Roots die and bare soil is left, which is easily removed by wind or water.
2. **Ploughing up and down slopes**. Water runs down the furrows and carries soil away.	2. **Overcropping**. Too much goodness taken out of soil by crops and not put back with fertilisers. Soil becomes useless and can easily be eroded.
	3. **Ploughing in semi-arid areas**. Grass cover removed and soil blows away in dry periods.

Water erosion is found on slopes.
Wind erosion is found on slopes and flat land.

▲ **4.11a** Causes of soil erosion

▼ **4.11b** Areas of severe soil erosion in the USA

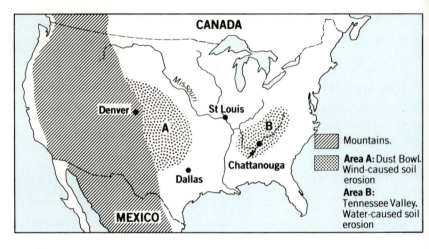

◄ **4.12** Prevention of soil erosion

Terracing slopes. Stops water running down. Water carried down the 'steps' by drains.
Contour ploughing. Ploughing across the slopes. Water collects in furrows and does not run down.

Putting back a vegetation cover. Protects the soil with grass or trees. Stops soil being washed or blown away.
Strip cropping. Growing crops in strips separated by permanent strips of grass. Stops wind erosion.
Mulching. Covering any bare soil between plants with straw. Stops wind erosion.

▼ **4.13a** China clay

Weathering: good or bad?

Weathering forms soil in which we grow food. It also breaks up our roads and rots our buildings, costing millions of pounds to repair each year. There is also increasing evidence that chemical weathering which results from pollution is causing great damage to the environment. 4.13a, b, c show three other ways in which weathering can affect us.

In 4.13a, a jet of water is blasted at chemically weathered granite in Cornwall. Granite is made up of three minerals: quartz, felspar and mica. Felspar and mica rot down to form white china clay. The clay is carried off by the water and settled out in tanks. Examples of uses are for pottery and for coating paper.

When some rocks (especially chalk and limestone) are chemically weathered, chemicals are carried away by rainwater. These chemicals build up inside water mains (4.13b) and reduce the water flow. Similar deposits also occur in boilers and kettles and are known as *scale*.

In 4.13c bauxite is being dug from the lower layers of soil in Jamaica. In tropical hot wet areas chemical weathering breaks up rock and some metal ores are washed downwards (leached). Bauxite is rich in aluminium which is used for such things as aeroplane bodies and saucepans.

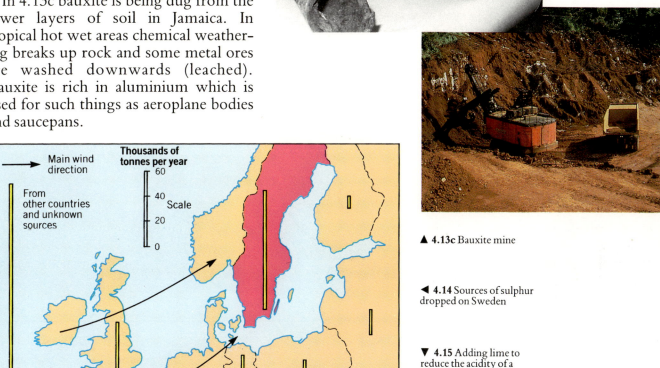

◀ **4.13b** Furred-up pipes

▲ **4.13c** Bauxite mine

◀ **4.14** Sources of sulphur dropped on Sweden

▼ **4.15** Adding lime to reduce the acidity of a Swedish lake

Thousands of tonnes per year

Main wind direction

From other countries and unknown sources

60
40 Scale
20
0

Acid rain

Fumes from factories and power stations contain sulphur dioxide which turns rain into very dilute sulphuric acid (**acid rain**). This acid rain is very destructive to plants, and makes rivers and lakes unable to support life. 4.14 shows how winds carry sulphur from many countries to Sweden. The acid rain which falls there makes trees grow more slowly and reduces crop yields. 4.15 shows a Swedish lake having lime added to it to try to neutralise the acid which is killing fish.

5   Back to the sea

Weathering softens and weakens the surface of rocks. The loosened material is then removed and begins a long journey to the sea. The process of removal is called **erosion**. 5.1a–d show the four methods at work. 5.1e shows gravity playing its part as material slides or falls down slopes. The eroded material rests many times on its way to the sea. For millions of years it is **deposited** in deep ocean basins called **geosynclines**. How **convection current** movements cause these **sediments** to form **fold mountains** is explained on 3.14b on page 16. As soon as the newly folded sedimentary rocks emerge from the sea, weathering and erosion begin again. 5.2 shows how weathering, erosion, transport, deposition and mountain building join together to form the **rock cycle**.

▼ **5.1** How is it moved?

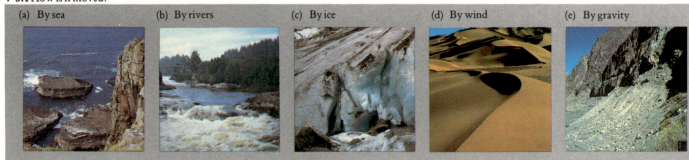

(a) By sea   (b) By rivers   (c) By ice   (d) By wind   (e) By gravity

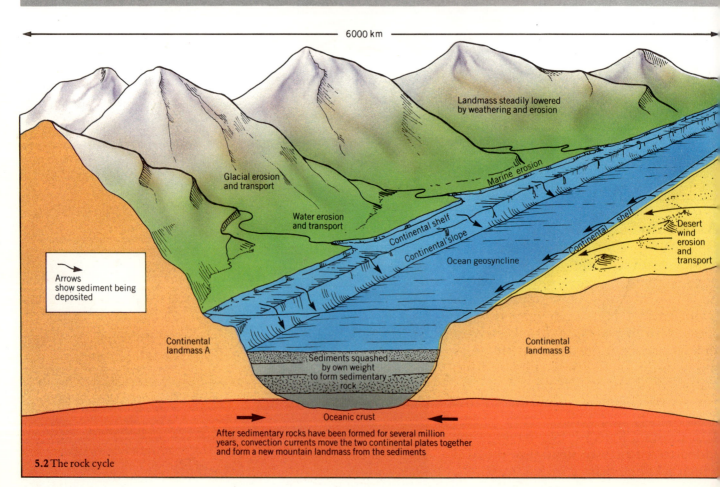

6000 km

Landmass steadily lowered by weathering and erosion

Glacial erosion and transport

Marine erosion

Water erosion and transport

Continental shelf

Continental slope

Ocean geosyncline

Continental shelf

Desert wind erosion and transport

Arrows show sediment being deposited

Continental landmass A

Continental landmass B

Sediments squashed by own weight to form sedimentary rock

Oceanic crust

After sedimentary rocks have been formed for several million years, convection currents move the two continental plates together and form a new mountain landmass from the sediments

5.2 The rock cycle

6 Fast and slow

What's it all about?

The movement of weathered material (**debris**) down a slope by the pull of gravity is called **mass movement**. The debris may be removed from the bottom of the slope by **erosion** (for example, by rivers). How fast and how suddenly the movement takes place depends on a number of things.

- *The angle of slope:* the steeper the angle the greater the pull of gravity and the faster the movement.

- *The vegetation cover:* grass or tree roots will bind debris and therefore prevent or slow movement.

- *Rainfall:* mass movement is faster in wet weather. Debris soaks up rainwater, becoming heavier, so the pull of gravity is more. Also, if water cannot pass through the rock below the debris, it flows down the rock surface helping movement of the debris.

Dangerously fast

6.1 shows the different ways in which fast movement of debris can occur. All of these ways can be dangerous. 6.2 shows what happened after heavy rain in Baños in Spain when a landslide carried away much of the road. Luckily no-one was hurt. In 1966, however, 144 people were killed at Aberfan in South Wales when a sudden mudflow from a saturated coal tip covered the village school.

◀ **6.2** Landslide at Baños in Spain

▼ **6.1** Rapid movements of weathered rock

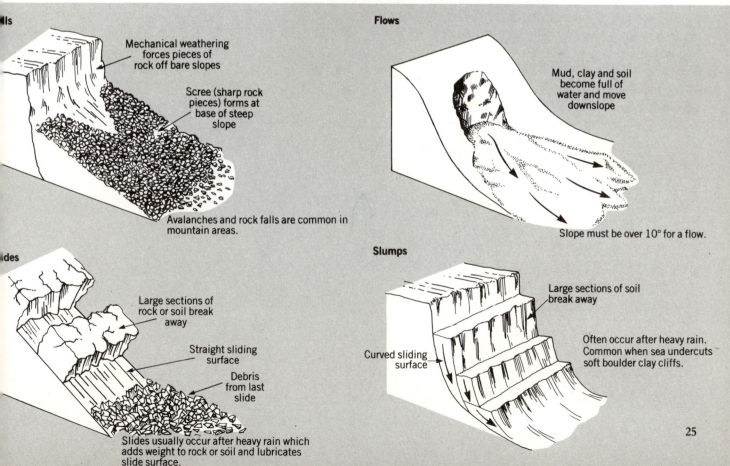

Falls

Mechanical weathering forces pieces of rock off bare slopes

Scree (sharp rock pieces) forms at base of steep slope

Avalanches and rock falls are common in mountain areas.

Flows

Mud, clay and soil become full of water and move downslope

Slope must be over 10° for a flow.

Slides

Large sections of rock or soil break away

Straight sliding surface

Debris from last slide

Slides usually occur after heavy rain which adds weight to rock or soil and lubricates slide surface.

Slumps

Large sections of soil break away

Often occur after heavy rain. Common when sea undercuts soft boulder clay cliffs.

Curved sliding surface

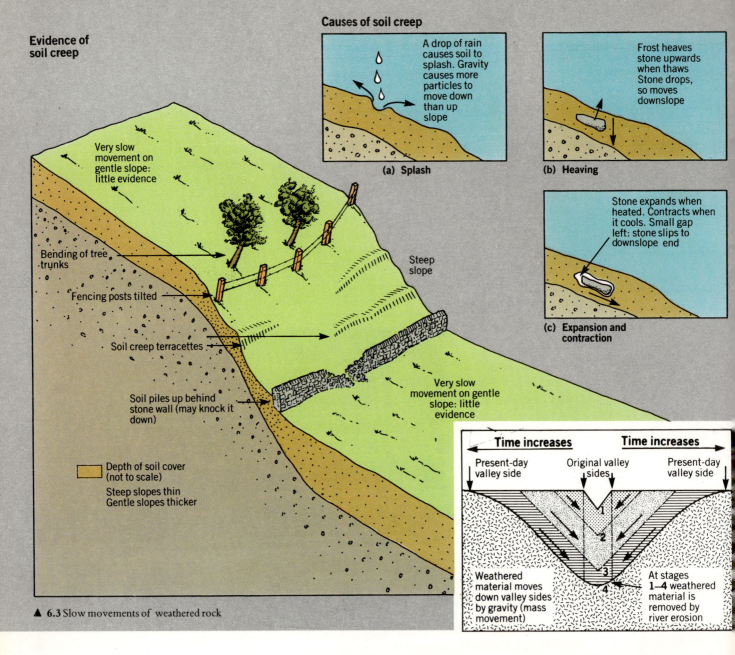

Evidence of soil creep

Very slow movement on gentle slope: little evidence

Bending of tree trunks

Fencing posts tilted

Soil creep terracettes

Soil piles up behind stone wall (may knock it down)

Steep slope

Very slow movement on gentle slope: little evidence

Depth of soil cover (not to scale)
Steep slopes thin
Gentle slopes thicker

▲ **6.3** Slow movements of weathered rock

Causes of soil creep

A drop of rain causes soil to splash. Gravity causes more particles to move down than up slope

(a) Splash

Frost heaves stone upwards when thaws Stone drops, so moves downslope

(b) Heaving

Stone expands when heated. Contracts when it cools. Small gap left: stone slips to downslope end

(c) Expansion and contraction

Time increases ← → Time increases

Present-day valley side

Original valley sides

Present-day valley side

Weathered material moves down valley sides by gravity (mass movement)

At stages 1–4 weathered material is removed by river erosion

▲ **6.4** Mass movement shaping valley form

Slow and sure

Slow mass movement or **soil creep** is so slow that it cannot be seen. It is a flow movement where the bits of soil move individually. 6.3 shows the tell-tale signs of soil creep and explains how this movement is brought about. Large amounts of soil move down slopes in this way. Removal of trees or grass from a slope can be dangerous. The binding effect of roots is lost and rapid mass movement and water erosion (see page 22) can quickly remove much of the soil.

Keeping pace

6.4 shows how mass movement and erosion work together to form a valley. For thousands of years weathered rock moves down the sides and is removed by a river. If the river cannot keep pace, this balance will be upset and valley development will slow. When the river is unable to erode, debris builds up and protects the sides from further weathering. Then the valley does not widen or deepen further.

7   Running water

A vital substance

Water is a vital substance in all our lives. Each person must drink about 10 times their own weight of water each year. But this is only a small amount of the water used by people. 7.1 lists the amounts of water needed to make a number of products, and shows how much each person uses in the home each day.

Water provides the cheapest way of transporting heavy and bulky goods such as coal. Rivers are therefore often important routeways (for example, the Rhine). Their courses may have to be straightened, or their beds deepened, to allow barges and boats to move. Where rivers are not suitable, canals may be built. Water can also be used to make **hydro-electric power**. In mountainous areas with heavy rainfall, dams can be built to collect river water in large reservoirs. The power of the water is then used to make electricity in power houses at the base of the dams. Huge amounts of water are also needed in **thermal** and **nuclear power stations**, both to make steam and for cooling. In many countries **irrigation** water is vital if crops are to be grown.

Industrial uses	
Product	Amount of water needed to make product
A car	40 000 litres
1 tonne of steel	134 000 litres
A bicycle	170 litres
1 litre of beer	8.6 litres
1 kg loaf of bread	1.4 litres

Household uses	
Use	Amount of water per person per day
Hose pipes outside home	3 litres
Clothes washing machine	13 litres
Toilet flushing	36 litres
Baths and showers	20 litres
Other uses	40 litres
Total	**112 litres**

▲ **7.1** Uses of water

Caring for water

With such a great need for water, all supplies must be cared for. Polluted rivers and lakes cannot be used by people. River life also suffers. In 7.2 the different pollution levels along the River Tame are shown.

▼ **7.2** Pollution along the River Tame

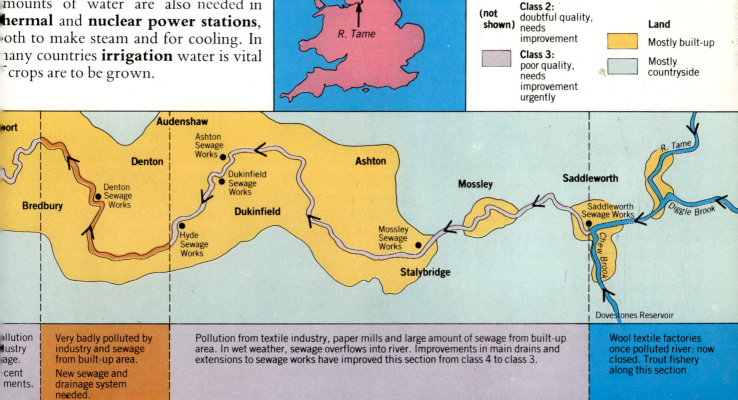

Location of R. Tame

Water quality

| Class 1: unpolluted and clear |
| Class 4: very badly polluted |

(not shown) Class 2: doubtful quality, needs improvement

Class 3: poor quality, needs improvement urgently

Land
Mostly built-up
Mostly countryside

Pollution industry age. cent ments. | Very badly polluted by industry and sewage from built-up area. New sewage and drainage system needed. | Pollution from textile industry, paper mills and large amount of sewage from built-up area. In wet weather, sewage overflows into river. Improvements in main drains and extensions to sewage works have improved this section from class 4 to class 3. | Wool textile factories once polluted river: now closed. Trout fishery along this section.

Too much or too little

Floods, such as those shown in 7.3 near Tewkesbury (Gloucestershire), can damage farmland, block roads and railways, and kill animals or even people. Too little rain to fill rivers and reservoirs can also cause problems. 7.4 shows a reservoir near Aldershot during the 1976 drought. Water had to be strictly rationed in many parts of Britain, and watering gardens and washing cars was banned. To avoid damage or hardship it is therefore very important to understand changes in flow rates of rivers and other water supplies.

How much flows?

Careful study of 7.5a and b shows that, while there is a link between the amount of rainfall and river flow, river levels do not increase *immediately* after rain. There is a time lag between the peak rainfall and peak flow. Water takes time to wet the **vegetation** and ground, and then pass through the soil and rocks to the river. 7.5c shows the normal pattern. However, the amount of rainfall is not the only factor which decides flow levels. Others are outlined in 7.5d.

▲ 7.3 Tewkesbury floods

▼ 7.4 Empty reservoir near Aldershot

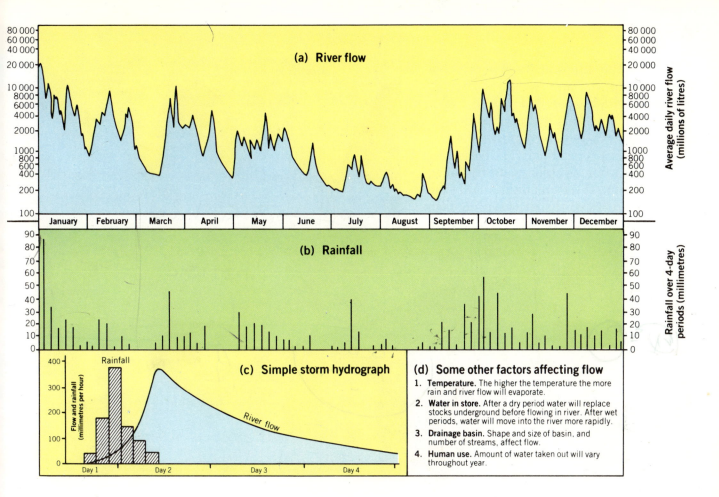

(a) River flow

Average daily river flow (millions of litres)

January | February | March | April | May | June | July | August | September | October | November | December

(b) Rainfall

Rainfall over 4-day periods (millimetres)

(c) Simple storm hydrograph

Flow and rainfall (millimetres per hour)

Rainfall

River flow

Day 1 | Day 2 | Day 3 | Day 4

(d) Some other factors affecting flow

1. **Temperature.** The higher the temperature the more rain and river flow will evaporate.
2. **Water in store.** After a dry period water will replace stocks underground before flowing in river. After wet periods, water will move into the river more rapidly.
3. **Drainage basin.** Shape and size of basin, and number of streams, affect flow.
4. **Human use.** Amount of water taken out will vary throughout year.

Energy levels

The amount of work done by rivers in shaping the landscape depends upon their **energy** levels. A river's energy depends upon its *volume* (amount of water) and its *velocity* (speed of flow). Increases in volume or velocity produce more energy. Whenever the river in-creases its energy, it can transport more material and erode more of its bed and banks. When energy decreases, less material can be carried. Part of the load will be dropped (**deposition**) and **erosion** will slow or stop. 7.6 shows how friction with the bed and banks, and the shape of the river channel, can affect energy levels.

▲ **7.5** River flow and rainfall on part of the River Ribble

▼ **7.6a** Flow in stream channels

▼ **7.6b** Stream channel efficiency

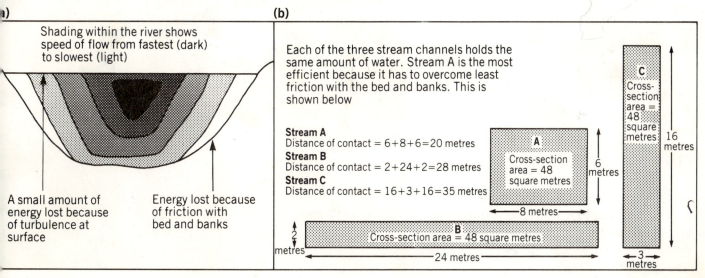

(a)

Shading within the river shows speed of flow from fastest (dark) to slowest (light)

A small amount of energy lost because of turbulence at surface

Energy lost because of friction with bed and banks

(b)

Each of the three stream channels holds the same amount of water. Stream A is the most efficient because it has to overcome least friction with the bed and banks. This is shown below

Stream A
Distance of contact = 6+8+6=20 metres
Stream B
Distance of contact = 2+24+2=28 metres
Stream C
Distance of contact = 16+3+16=35 metres

A
Cross-section area = 48 square metres
6 metres
8 metres

B
Cross-section area = 48 square metres
2 metres
24 metres

C
Cross-section area = 48 square metres
16 metres
3 metres

A typical river

7.7 shows the different ways in which a river transports and erodes material. Material which is eroded in the upper part of the course is transported downstream, where it will be deposited.

7.8 shows a typical drainage basin of a large river. For simplicity, it has been divided into three sections, and the general features of the river within each section are shown. In reality, things are

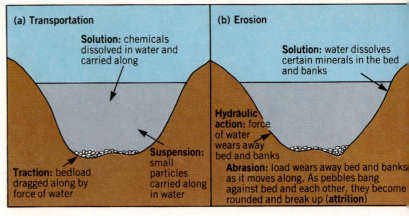

(a) Transportation

Solution: chemicals dissolved in water and carried along

Traction: bedload dragged along by force of water

Suspension: small particles carried along in water

(b) Erosion

Solution: water dissolves certain minerals in the bed and banks

Hydraulic action: force of water wears away bed and banks

Abrasion: load wears away bed and banks as it moves along. As pebbles bang against bed and each other, they become rounded and break up (**attrition**)

▲ **7.7** How a river transports and erodes

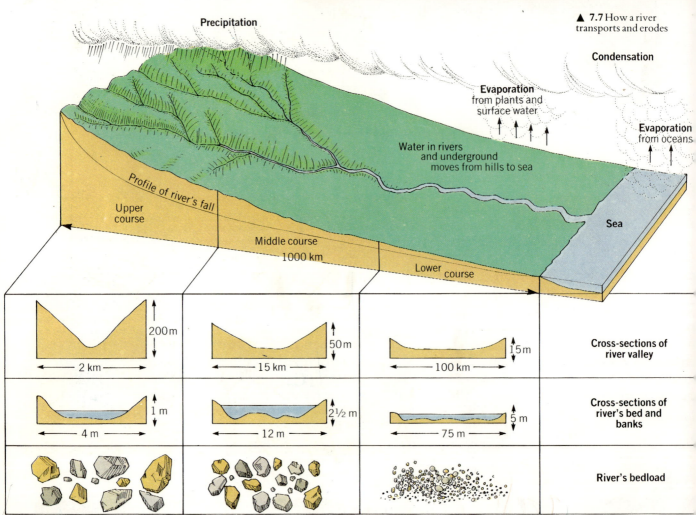

▲ **7.8** Features of a river

▼ **7.9** Upper course river

more complicated than this. Changes in rock type, different human activities, differences in **climate** and other factors can all have important effects.

Vertical erosion (wearing downwards) is important in the upper course, producing the steep sides and narrow valley floor shown in 7.9. The river is usually narrow and often shallow. It falls steeply and unevenly. Most work is done in times of flood when small rocks swirled in whirlpools (caused by uneven depth) drill into the bed, forming potholes. Large boulders in the bed are only moved in extreme flood conditions.

Where a resistant layer of rock slows erosion, a waterfall may form as shown in 7.10. As this erodes back, a gorge may be produced. An upper course river moves from side to side as it cuts its valley, forming **interlocking spurs** (7.12c).

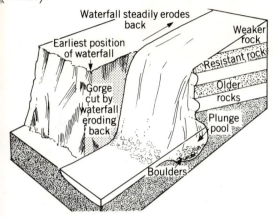

7.10 Formation of a waterfall and gorge

7.11 shows a typical scene in the middle course where the river is wider and deeper. There is still some vertical erosion, but **lateral** (sideways) **erosion** is the most important. As the river swings from side to side, erosion takes place on the outside of the bends, where the current is fastest (7.12a). Deposition occurs on the inside of the bend as shown in 7.12a and b. Steadily the interlocking spurs are worn back, and the **meanders** themselves move downstream (7.12c-e). Eventually the meandering river flows across a **flood plain**, bordered by a line of **bluffs** (7.12f). The valley sides are steadily lowered and become less steep. 7.12g shows how meanders can move downstream to widen the flood plain over a period of time.

7.11 Middle course river   ▶ **7.12** Lateral erosion by a river

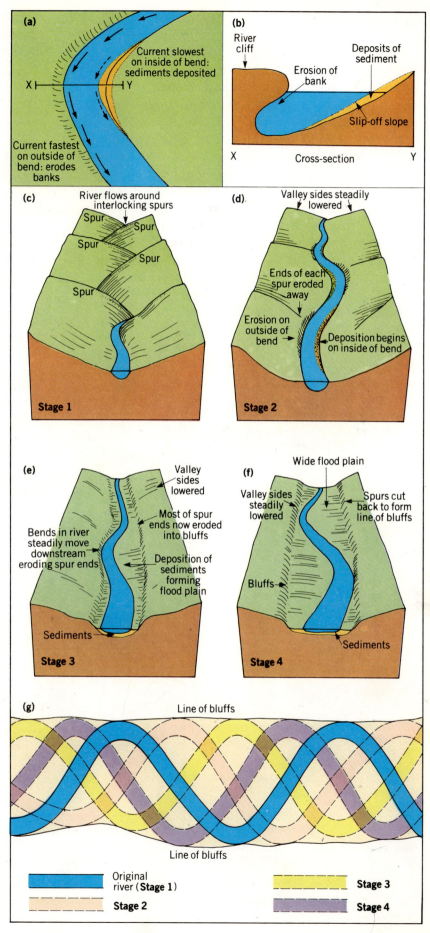

(a) Current slowest on inside of bend: sediments deposited

X ⊢ Y

Current fastest on outside of bend: erodes banks

(b) River cliff — Erosion of bank — Deposits of sediment — Slip-off slope

X   Cross-section   Y

(c) River flows around interlocking spurs

Spur Spur Spur Spur Spur

Stage 1

(d) Valley sides steadily lowered — Ends of each spur eroded away — Erosion on outside of bend — Deposition begins on inside of bend

Stage 2

(e) Valley sides lowered — Bends in river steadily move downstream eroding spur ends — Most of spur ends now eroded into bluffs — Deposition of sediments forming flood plain — Sediments

Stage 3

(f) Wide flood plain — Valley sides steadily lowered — Spurs cut back to form line of bluffs — Bluffs — Sediments

Stage 4

(g) Line of bluffs — Line of bluffs

| Original river (**Stage 1**) | | Stage 3 |
| Stage 2 | | Stage 4 |

A typical lower course river, shown in 7.13, is wide and deep, meandering wildly over a large flat flood plain. Valley sides are low and very gently sloping. Huge quantities of **sediments** which have been carried downstream are deposited. 7.14 shows how such a river can change its course and form **oxbow lakes**.

The flood plain may be tens of kilometres wide, and will be flooded if the river breaks through its banks. A fine covering of material will be left, thickest near the river. In time, **levees** (small mounds) of this material may be left on each bank. People can reinforce these to prevent further floods. The sediments also provide rich soil for farmers.

Millions of tonnes of sediment will be dumped into the sea each year by a large river. If the sediment is deposited faster than tides and currents remove it, new land will be made as a **delta**. Two types of delta are shown in 7.15a and b. However, if powerful tides or currents remove sediments faster than they are deposited, **estuaries** may form (7.15c) and, if the level of the sea rises, the valley floor may be drowned.

◀ **7.13** Lower course river

▼ **7.14** Formation of oxbow lakes

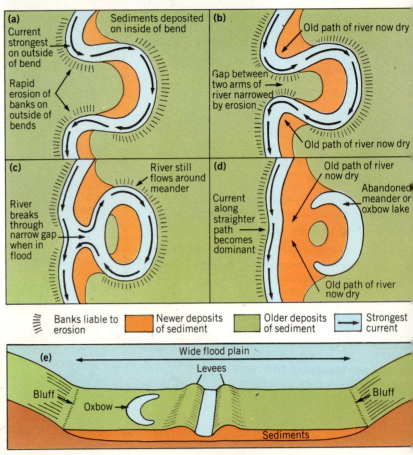

(a) Current strongest on outside of bend — Sediments deposited on inside of bend — Rapid erosion of banks on outside of bends

(b) Old path of river now dry — Gap between two arms of river narrowed by erosion — Old path of river now dry

(c) River breaks through narrow gap when in flood — River still flows around meander

(d) Current along straighter path becomes dominant — Old path of river now dry — Abandoned meander or oxbow lake — Old path of river now dry

Banks liable to erosion | Newer deposits of sediment | Older deposits of sediment | Strongest current

(e) Wide flood plain — Levees — Bluff — Oxbow — Bluff — Sediments

▼ **7.15** Where rivers meet the sea

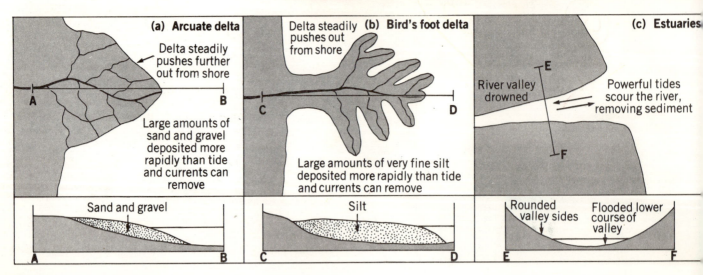

(a) Arcuate delta
Delta steadily pushes further out from shore
A ——— B
Large amounts of sand and gravel deposited more rapidly than tide and currents can remove
Sand and gravel
A ——— B

(b) Bird's foot delta
Delta steadily pushes out from shore
C ——— D
Large amounts of very fine silt deposited more rapidly than tide and currents can remove
Silt
C ——— D

(c) Estuaries
River valley drowned
Powerful tides scour the river, removing sediment
E — F
Rounded valley sides — Flooded lower course of valley
E ——— F

Too little rain

Where rainfall is low, or comes only in one season, rivers often dry up completely (7.16). Water can sometimes be found underground, however. 7.17 shows how **artesian basins** can be valuable sources of water.

Even in dry areas, rivers play an important part in shaping the landscape. 7.18 outlines some of the most important features produced. Rivers such as the Colorado (USA) flow from wetter areas into an **arid** zone, cutting deep steep-sided valleys such as the Grand Canyon. Water from elsewhere provides the power for vertical erosion, but there is little rain to lower the valley sides by speeding up **weathering** and **mass movement** (see page 25).

Following periods of rain, which are often very heavy, huge quantities of water meet in the valley bottom, causing **flash floods**. Deep valleys called **wadis** and smaller gullies are formed.

Tonnes of deposited material may form at the foot of slopes, and deposits build up over the valley floor. Inland lakes form which evaporate rapidly if temperatures are high, leaving minerals and salt deposits.

◀ **7.16** Dried-up river bed

▼ **7.17** Artesian basins

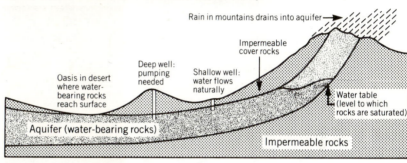

Rain in mountains drains into aquifer

Impermeable cover rocks

Oasis in desert where water-bearing rocks reach surface

Deep well: pumping needed

Shallow well: water flows naturally

Water table (level to which rocks are saturated)

Aquifer (water-bearing rocks)

Impermeable rocks

➤ **7.18** Water in arid areas

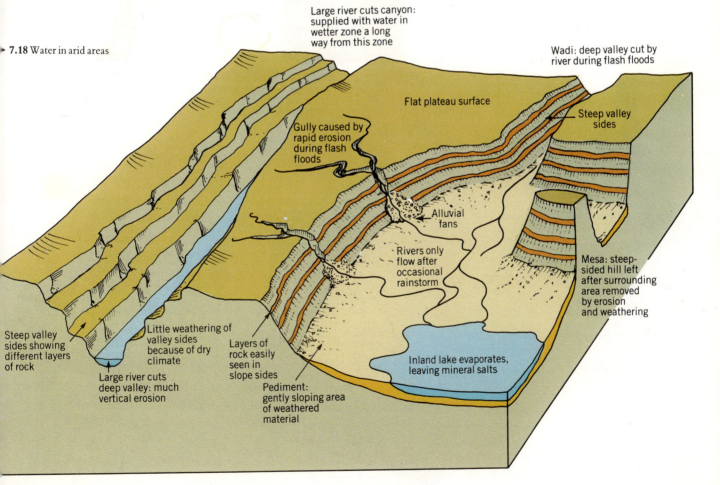

Large river cuts canyon: supplied with water in wetter zone a long way from this zone

Wadi: deep valley cut by river during flash floods

Flat plateau surface

Gully caused by rapid erosion during flash floods

Steep valley sides

Alluvial fans

Rivers only flow after occasional rainstorm

Mesa: steep-sided hill left after surrounding area removed by erosion and weathering

Steep valley sides showing different layers of rock

Little weathering of valley sides because of dry climate

Layers of rock easily seen in slope sides

Large river cuts deep valley: much vertical erosion

Pediment: gently sloping area of weathered material

Inland lake evaporates, leaving mineral salts

Eating rocks away

Landscapes produced by rivers vary with different types of rocks. The effect of rivers on limestone produces some fascinating landscapes. All limestones contain at least 50% calcium carbonate. Rainwater passing through the atmosphere and soil picks up small amounts of carbon dioxide, turning into very dilute carbonic acid. This can react with calcium carbonate making it soluble.

Most water passes through lines of weakness in the limestone: either **bedding planes**, which divide different layers; or **joints** which are vertical weaknesses. Most **solution**, therefore, occurs along these lines making many limestone features block shaped.

Rivers rarely flow on the surface in limestone areas. They disappear down **swallow holes**, where joints and bedding planes have been eaten away. Water then passes through a complicated system of underground caves and passages. 7.19 shows how calcium carbonate has been deposited on the roof, forming stalactites, and on the floor, forming stalagmites.

Water moves downwards until it reaches **impermeable** rocks, through which it cannot pass. It then makes its way to the surface, reappearing as a spring. The major features of limestone areas are shown in 7.20. The inset shows a typical **limestone pavement**. Solution has eaten along the joints and bedding planes. Also noticeable on 7.20 are **dry valleys**. These may once have been caves whose roofs have now collapsed. Or they may be a relic of a time when it was much wetter, or when joints were frozen and rivers could flow on the surface.

◄ **7.19** Underground limestone features

Gryke
Clint
Joint
Bedding plane

Detail of limestone pavement

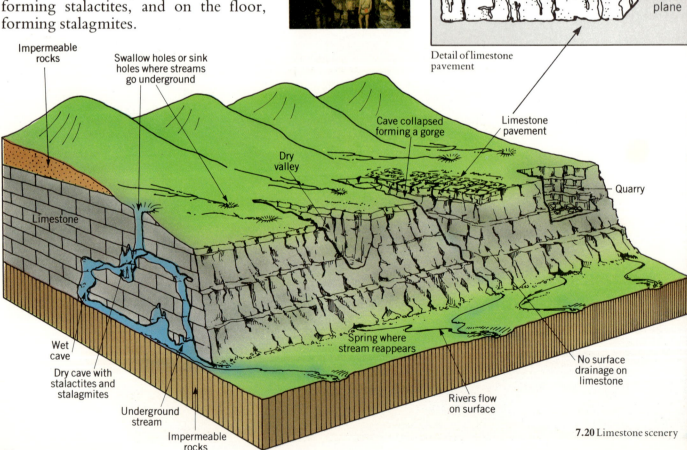

Impermeable rocks

Swallow holes or sink holes where streams go underground

Cave collapsed forming a gorge

Dry valley

Limestone pavement

Quarry

Limestone

Wet cave

Dry cave with stalactites and stalagmites

Underground stream

Impermeable rocks

Spring where stream reappears

Rivers flow on surface

No surface drainage on limestone

7.20 Limestone scenery

Chalk and clay

Dry valleys also occur in chalk (7.21). Chalk is a special type of limestone, not as resistant as the carboniferous limestone found in places such as the Peak District. It contains many fewer joints, and forms the more rounded landscapes of areas like the South Downs.

7.22 is a typical scene in a chalk area. There is rarely any surface drainage; water seeps underground through solution holes. Caves are not usually formed because the water passes through pores (small holes) in the chalk. If an impermeable rock such as clay lies under the chalk, water will collect in the chalk layer. The level to which the chalk is *saturated* is called the **water table**. This varies in height with the rainfall. Rocks such as clay are more easily eroded than chalk, and form flat lowland areas. At the junction of the chalk and clay a line of springs appears, at the same level as the water table. Springs were very important in the past when people had to live next to sources of water. Villages were sited near them.

Chalk often forms a steep **scarp slope** running across the landscape, behind which is a more gentle **dip slope**. In the past, this was used almost entirely for grazing but, as farming methods have improved, many chalk areas are now cultivated.

Limestone areas attract many tourists, because they provide interesting and sometimes spectacular upland scenery. They can be used for a wide variety of leisure activities, including pot-holing, walking and pony trekking.

◀ **7.21** Dry valley

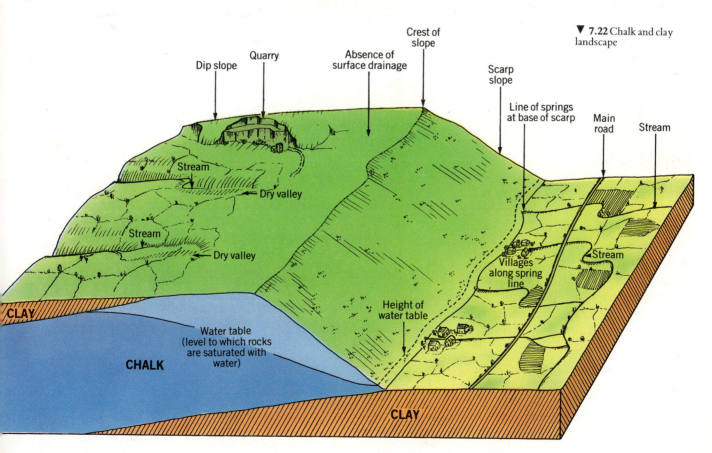

▼ **7.22** Chalk and clay landscape

8 Ice

What next?

Britain was once much colder than it is now. An Ice Age may never happen again, but we cannot be certain. Temperatures change not only from season to season, but from year to year and century to century. Temperatures may fall again and, if they do, most of Britain would be covered in ice. If temperatures rise (which is also possible), ice at the poles would melt, causing the sea level to rise and possibly flood many lowland areas of Britain. The graphs in 8.1 show past temperature changes.

▼ 8.1 Changes in Britain's temperature

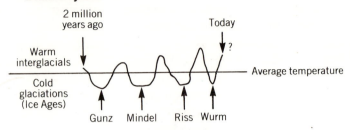

(a) Temperature changes over the last 2 million years

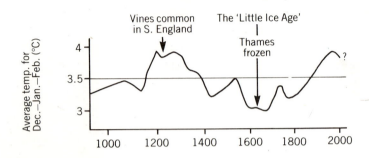

(b) Winter temperature changes over the last 1000 years

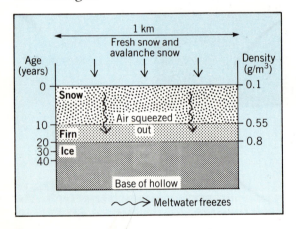

▲ 8.2 Ice formation on a Swiss rock hollow

Forming ice

If winter snowfall is not removed by the warmth of summer it builds up in hollows and forms ice (8.2). As the ice starts to move downslope under its own weight the hollows are enlarged and deepened by **erosion** (8.3). Erosion is by **plucking** and **abrasion**. Rock is plucked when water freezes around a bit of rock which sticks out. The water also freezes to the main body of ice and as the ice moves the rock is snapped off. Plucking is very important at the back of the hollow. Plucking and **mechanical weathering** by **freeze–thaw** (see 4.2) cause a steep back wall or

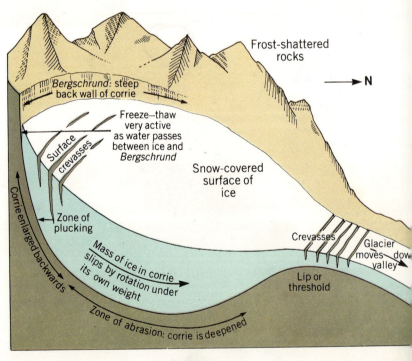

▲ 8.3 Corrie formation

bergschrund to form. In abrasion the plucked pieces sticking out of the base of the ice scratch and grind the rock below like a giant piece of sandpaper. The ice moves out of the much bigger hollow (now called a **corrie**) as a **valley glacier**.

8.4 shows a mountainous area with some snow and ice, as it looks today. It is easy to imagine the area being heavily glaciated when temperatures were lower. 8.5 gives some common clues that show **glacial erosion** has taken place. The steep-sided corries may contain a small lake or **tarn** held back by a lip of rock called the **threshold** (8.3). Two corries side by side are separated by a steep ridge called an **arête**, and a **horn** may be seen where corries are found on all sides of a mountain. Lower down, the shape of the valley is a good guide. 8.6 shows the differences between a water-formed and an ice-formed valley. Some glacial valleys contain long thin lakes called **ribbon lakes**. Bare rocks in glacial valleys often show scratch marks (**striations**) caused by abrasion.

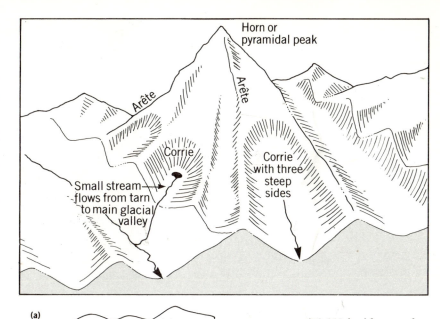

▲ 8.5 Upland features of glacial erosion

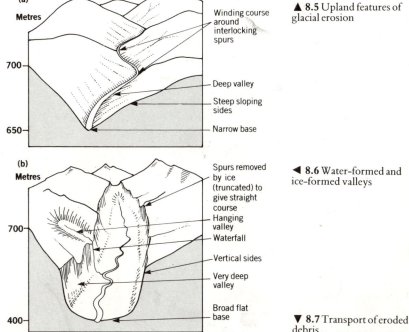

◀ 8.6 Water-formed and ice-formed valleys

▼ 8.4 Upland glaciated scenery

▼ 8.7 Transport of eroded debris

Transport

8.7 shows how a glacier moves eroded **debris**. All material carried on, in or under the ice is called **moraine**. Plucking gives sharp fragments of all shapes and sizes. Freeze–thaw provides similar material from the slopes above the glacier. Abrasion forms clay-sized particles called **rock flour**. Much debris is carried by streams under the glacier.

Most glaciers move less than 1 metre a day. The rate of flow is linked to the supply of ice from the corrie and to the steepness of slope.

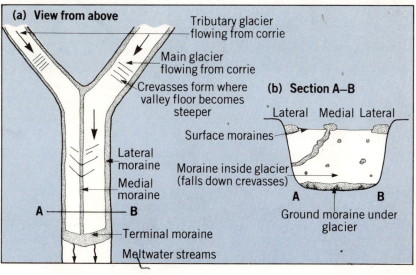

The snout

The melting ice in 8.8 looks like the face of a dog and, by chance, the place where the glacier ends is called the **snout**. Meltwater from under the ice and snout forms fast-flowing streams. The melting ice is old and dirty after its long journey from one or more corries. The snout advances or retreats depending on the amount of ice being supplied higher up and temperature changes at the snout. Material deposited by ice upstream is very different from water-deposited debris downstream of the snout.

▲ 8.8 The snout of a glacier

Sorting it out

8.9 shows how sheets, ridges and mounds are deposited by ice and meltwater. Ice drops unsorted debris of all shapes and sizes: this is called boulder clay or **till**. Water rounds the debris and sorts it by size. The heaviest is dropped nearest the snout and the lightest clay-sized particles are carried furthest away. 8.10 shows how the two types of deposit are linked to the features of 8.9. The **terminal moraine ridge** is the furthest point down the valley reached by the glacier. **Erratics** are not shown in 8.9. They are large and small rocks dropped by ice. Tracing their origins tells us about the direction of ice movement. Ice sheets covered large parts of Northern Europe during the last Ice Age and glacial deposits cover much of the solid rock of the area.

▼ 8.9 A landscape of glacial deposition

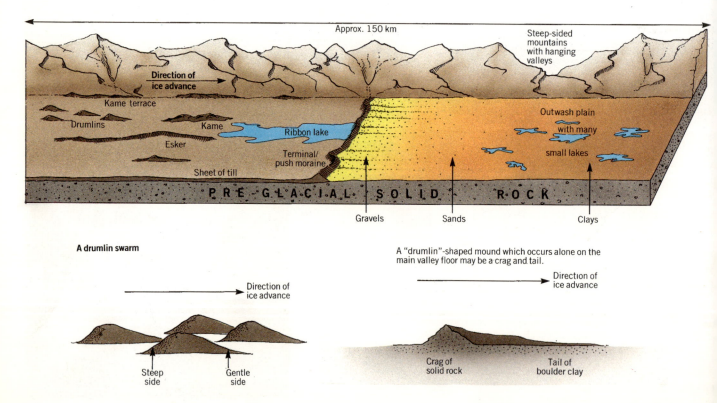

All material carried on, in or under ice is deposited as:

unsorted boulder clay or till.

Rock flour

Angular pieces of rock

OR **sorted** by water into:

Pieces become rounded

Gravel and then deposited

Sand

Clay

Sheets. Dropped when ice retreats quickly. Many metres thick.	**Sheets.** Meltwater streams carry deposits away. Gravel dropped nearest ice front and small clay particles carried furthest.
Ridges. Across a valley. (i) **Terminal moraine.** Formed when snout of glacier stays in same place for tens of years. (10-400m high) (ii) **Push moraines.** Look like (i). Formed when ice moves forward again after retreating and pushes up sheet deposits.	**Ridges.** Along a valley. (i) **Eskers.** Long winding ridges of sand and gravel about 10m high. Formed by streams under the ice. (ii) **Kame terraces.** At side of valley. Formed by streams at side of glacier.
Mounds. Egg-shaped groups of hills up to 50m high. Formed under the ice. Called *drumlins*.	**Mounds.** Very uneven shapes found in valley. Formed by water under ice. Called *kames*

▼ **8.11** A Norwegian valley

Do we gain?

Much of Denmark is covered by **out-wash sands and clays** left by glacial deposition (see 8.9). In sandy areas plant food is quickly **leached** away (washed downwards by rain), but the wetter clay soil is more fertile. Fertilisers improve the quality of the sandy soil but clay soil till produces better crop yields.

Long straight glacial valley floors offer good farming land, communication routes and sites for settlement. The Norwegian valley floor in 8.11 stands out against the hostile mountains. Large dams built across some glacial valleys provide us with **hydro-electric power** (HEP) and with drinking water. Ribbon lakes help to make areas such as the Lake District attractive to tourists.

Ice melting at the end of the Ice Age caused the sea level to rise and drown low-lying glacial valleys. Nord **Fjord** in Norway (8.12) is typical. It gives sheltered deep-water anchorage for ships and, along with glaciers, offers spectacular scenery to tourists. Waterfalls caused by **hanging valleys** (see 8.6) provide Norway with much cheap HEP.

▶ **8.12** Nord Fjord

9 Wind and sea

Blowing sand

On 29 November 1979 many people in Lancaster, England, awoke to find their cars covered in a fine yellow-brown dust (9.1). The dust was traced to the Sahara of North West Africa. High-level winds carried the material over 2500 km, and rain caused it to fall to the ground. 9.2 shows how winds in a desert can lift fine dust high into the air.

Weathering in a desert (see page 18), produces rock fragments which can be

▲ **9.1** Saharan dust in Lancaster

Fine dust particles carried by even light winds up to hundreds of metres high. Fine particles blow round things and cause no erosion.

Wind usually

blows in

this direction

Undercutting of cliff face where sand grains are concentrated.

Sand grains lifted up to 2 metres above surface by strong winds: cause erosion as they bounce along.

Large particles roll along in very strong winds: no erosion.

◀ **9.2** Wind erosion and transport

moved by the force of wind. Movement is easy as there are so few plant roots to bind fragments together. As material is blown around, bits keep hitting each other, becoming broken up and rounded. 9.2 shows how the different-sized particles are affected by wind.

Blown sand causes **erosion** by **abrasion** seen as **undercutting** (9.2). 9.3 shows how this natural sand-blasting effect smooths and polishes rock. Weaknesses are picked out and in time only the most resistant sections are left: often as weird shapes. 9.4a, b and c show some minor and long-term effects of erosion. The wind deposits the sand as huge **sheets** or as **dunes**: two of the most common dune types are shown in 9.4d and e.

▼ **9.3** Natural sand-blasted rock

Wind erosion produces minor effects.

(a) Mushroom rocks

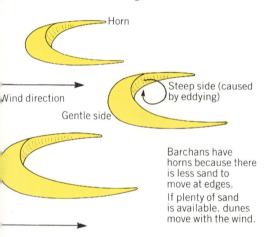

Hard rock

Band of soft rock gives much undercutting

Wind blows from many directions

0   3m

(b) Yardangs

Corridors cut by wind between hard rocks

Main wind direction

Hard rock

Soft rock

After long periods of weathering and erosion, residual features remain.

(c) Mesas and buttes
(Buttes are small mesas)

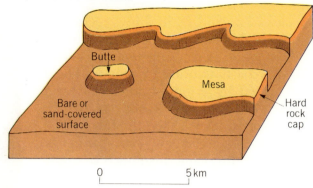

Butte

Mesa

Bare or sand-covered surface

Hard rock cap

0   5 km

Where the wind slackens, sand is dropped in regular-shaped dunes.

(d) Barchans   Maximum height 30 m

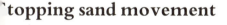

Horn

Wind direction

Gentle side

Steep side (caused by eddying)

Barchans have horns because there is less sand to move at edges.

If plenty of sand is available, dunes move with the wind.

(e) Seif dunes   (Longitudinal dunes)

May be several kilometres long and 15 m high

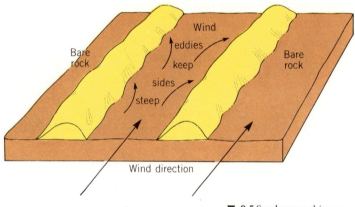

Bare rock

Wind eddies keep sides steep

Bare rock

Wind direction

▲ **9.4** Desert landscapes

▼ **9.5** Sand encroaching on an oasis

Stopping sand movement

Dust storms are a danger to desert travellers moving between settlements. Settlements are usually around an **oasis** where underground water reaches the surface. Moving sand may engulf an oasis, as is about to happen in 9.5. Planting bushes which can live with little water may help to stop this, so may building barriers. But, because the supply of sand is so great, some oases are lost and new ones formed each year.

Coastal dunes, which form when sand is blown off a beach, may move inland and invade good farmland. Dunes can be planted with marram grass to help stop this. It has a special root growth system to bind sand grains together.

Loss of land

Land is always being lost or gained from the sea. 9.6a shows erosion on the east coast of England. 9.6b shows reclaimed **deposited** material in the Netherlands.

The work of wearing away or building up coasts is done by waves. These are caused by winds, both locally and far out to sea. The distance over which the wind blows is called the **fetch**. The differences between **constructive** (coast-building) and **destructive** (coast-removing) waves is seen in 9.7. Destructive waves erode both loose beach material and weathered cliffs. Erosion types are shown in 9.8. The rate of erosion depends on the force of the waves, the rock hardness, the depth of water offshore, and the tidal power. For example, clay cliffs are eroded faster than chalk cliffs because clay is softer. 9.9 shows a coastline where a lot of erosion is taking place.

▲ **9.6a** Cliff erosion in eastern England

◀ **9.6b** Dutch polders

◀ **9.7** Types of waves

▶ **9.8** How the sea erodes

▼ **9.9** Features of coastal erosion

(a) Constructive waves

Beach material built up. Waves are gentle and occur 6-8 per minute

Strong **swash** pushes much material up beach

Weak **backwash** on surface: little loss of material

A lot of water drains back through beach material: no erosion

(b) Destructive waves

Beach material removed. Storm waves 12-14 per minute. Mainly occur in winter in Britain

Weak swash

Strong backwash on surface combs much material down beach

Little water drains back through beach material

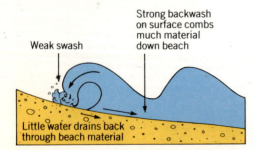

Hydraulic action. As waves pound rocks, air is trapped in cracks. When waves retreat, air expands violently and breaks off bits of rock.

Abrasion. Rock fragments are thrown at foot of cliffs by waves: bits of cliff are eroded. The size of rock fragments is reduced by them banging together and breaking (**attrition**).

Solution. Some rocks such as chalk and limestone slowly dissolve in sea water.

All three types of erosion cause undercutting of cliffs.

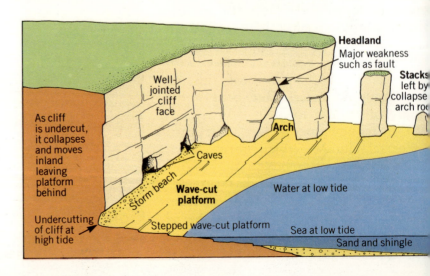

Headland

Major weakness such as fault

Stacks left by collapsed arch roof

Well-jointed cliff face

Arch

Caves

As cliff is undercut, it collapses and moves inland leaving platform behind

Storm beach

Wave-cut platform

Water at low tide

Undercutting of cliff at high tide

Stepped wave-cut platform

Sea at low tide

Sand and shingle

Undercutting at cliff bases shows rosion is greatest there. Weaknesses uch as cracks or **joints** are picked out y the sea, making the cliff line uneven nd causing **caves** in some rocks. Undercutting causes cliff collapse, orming a **wave-cut platform** (see .9). In time, waves lose much of their nergy in crossing the widening platorm so that cliff erosion slows or stops ltogether. When waves attack a **head-and** from both sides, **arches** may orm. Later, if the roof of the arch ollapses, a **stack** is left.

Eroded material may stay close to the liff from where it came. But often the and and shingle beneath a cliff (or overing parts of a platform) come from urther up the coast. This is due to **ongshore drift** shown in 9.10. Waves pproach the shore at an angle and naterial is moved along the coast by the **wash** and **backwash** of the waves (see .7).

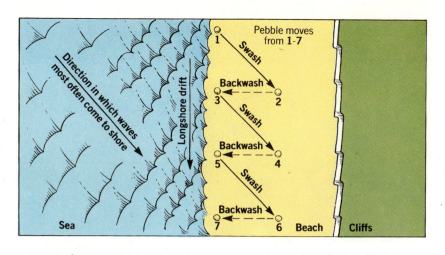

▲ **9.10** Longshore drift

Land is gained

When longshore drift is interrupted by a change in the direction of the coastline, or by a river entering the sea, **deposition** may occur. 9.11 shows **beaches, spits, tombolas, bars** and **lagoons**: all caused by deposition. Dunes form behind beaches, from blown sand. In time, plants take a hold in lagoons and new land is formed. Some areas of coastal deposition are attractive cheap sites for industry but it is for recreation that such areas are best known (9.11).

▼ **9.11** Features of coastal deposition

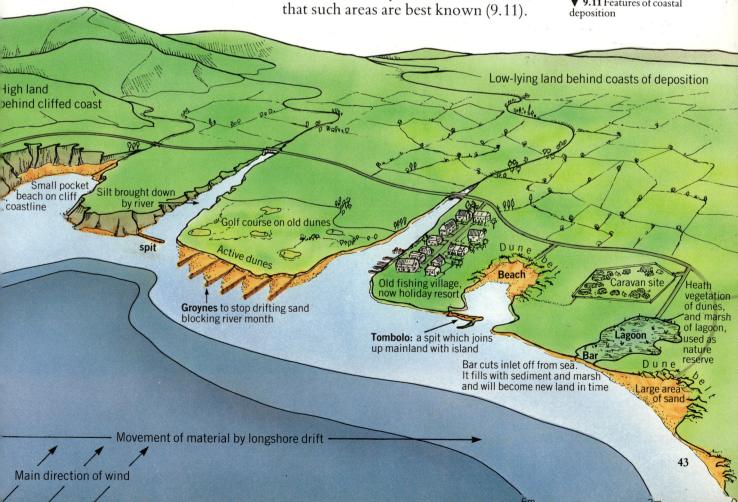

10.1a

10.1b

10.2 Hemispheres

Where am I?

The sailor shown in 10.1a could easily get lost on such a large expanse of ocean, but the latest electronic gadgets make it easier to find one's way. With the right equipment, the sailor could send a signal to a satellite (10.1b) which would immediately give the boat's exact position using **latitude** and **longitude**.

The earth is roughly a sphere, with the north and south poles at opposite ends. The circle which divides the earth into two halves, at an equal distance from each pole, forms two half spheres or hemispheres (10.2). This circle is the **equator**, and other circles parallel to it are called *lines of latitude* (10.3). Each line of latitude is identified by its angle in degrees north or south of the equator. A number of examples are shown in 10.3.

Another set of circles can be drawn which pass through the two poles (10.4). These are called **meridians** or *lines of longitude*. The line passing through Greenwich in London is taken to be 0°, and the line exactly on the other side of the world 180°. The lines of longitude are identified by their angles east or west of the **Greenwich meridian** as shown in 10.4.

10.3 Latitude

10.4 Longitude

Making it flat

For many years map-makers have faced the impossible task of making a map of a round world fit onto a flat piece of paper. Before the outer layer of a globe is stuck over its solid base it looks like 10.5. The gaps which appear when the globe is converted to a flat map are confusing. The only answer is to use a **map projection** which distorts the scale in some way. One of the most popular is the Mercator projection shown in 10.6. Areas around the equator are very accurate but, towards the poles, the areas of land shown on the map appear larger than they actually are.

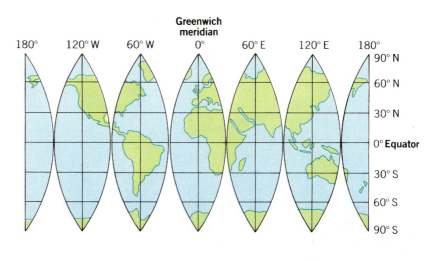

▲ **10.5** A peeled globe

▼ **10.6** The Mercator projection

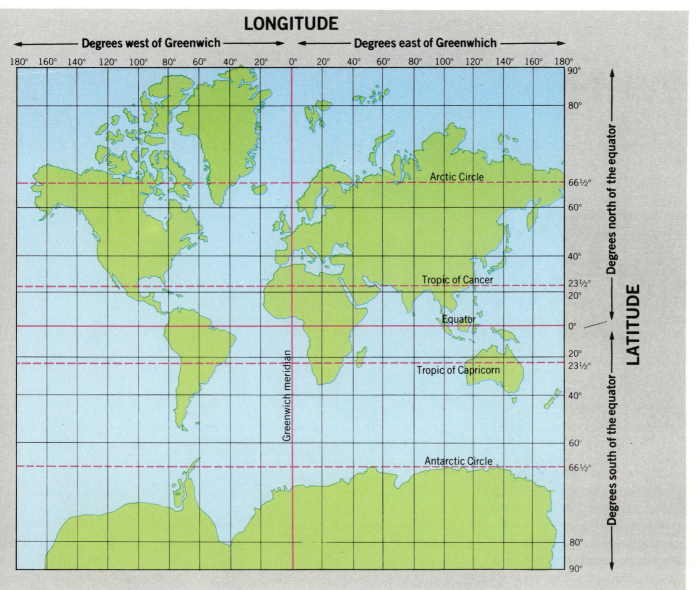

Light and dark

10.7 shows how the earth is tilted at an angle as it travels around the sun, and how only half of the planet can be in light at any time. The angle between different parts of the earth's surface and the mid-day sun, and the length of day and night, vary with the seasons. The detailed pattern is shown in 10.8.

The **Tropics of Cancer** and **Capricorn** mark the most northerly and southerly points reached by the overhead mid-day sun. The **Arctic** and **Antarctic Cirles** are the places furthest from the poles which have at least one 24-hour period each year with constant darkness, and one with constant light.

▶ **10.7** Day and night

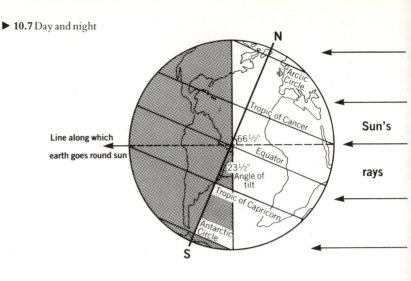

▼ **10.8** The seasons

The earth's orbit

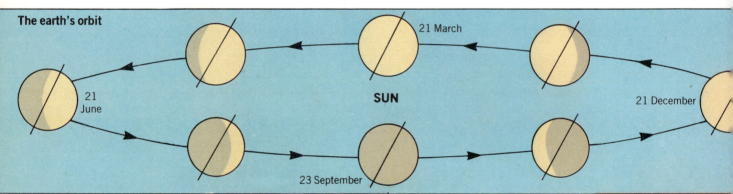

21 March

SUN

21 June

23 September

21 December

21 March spring equinox (northern)

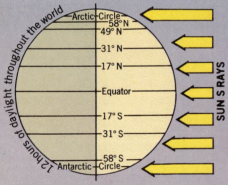

The mid-day sun is overhead at the equator.

Seasons
Spring in northern hemisphere.
Autumn in southern hemisphere.

Daylight hours
Equal throughout the world, so called **equinox**. 12 hours daylight and 12 hours night.

21 June summer solstice (northern)

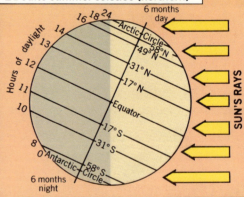

The mid-day sun overhead at Tropi Cancer

Seasons
Summer in north hemisphere. Win southern hemisph

Daylight hours
Northern hemisp long days and sho nights. Southern hemisphere has s days and long nig

23 September autumnal equinox (northern)

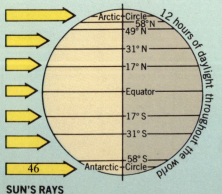

SUN'S RAYS

The mid-day sun is overhead at the equator.

Seasons
Spring in southern hemisphere. Autumn in northern hemisphere.

Daylight hours
Equal throughout the world. 12 hours daylight and 12 hours night.

21 December winter solstice (northern)

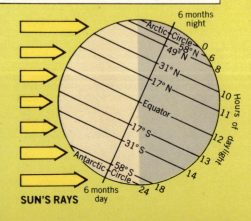

SUN'S RAYS

The mid-day sun overhead at Tropi Capricorn.

Seasons
Summer in south hemisphere. Win northern hemisph

Daylight hours
Southern hemisp long days and sho nights. Northern hemisphere has s days and long nig

46

On 21 March and 23 September the mid-day sun is overhead at the equator. These days are called **equinoxes**. All parts of the world have an equal amount of daylight and night.

21 June and 21 December are called **solstices**. On 21 June the mid-day sun is overhead at the Tropic of Cancer. The northern hemisphere has its summer with long hours of daylight. The southern hemisphere has its winter with long hours of night. On 21 December the mid-day sun is overhead at the Tropic of Capricorn. The northern hemisphere has its winter and the southern hemisphere has its summer.

What's the time?

At any point in time some parts of the world are in light and some are in darkness. In some places it is early morning and in others it is evening. The world is therefore divided into **time zones**, as shown in 10.9.

Lines of longitude are used (roughly) to mark the change from one time zone to the next. For every 15 degrees of longitude away from the Greenwich meridian (which is 0°) there is 1 hour time difference. To the east, time is ahead and, to the west, time is behind. Therefore at 60° W the time will be 4 hours behind Greenwich. If it is mid-day at 60° W, it will be 4 p.m. at Greenwich.

The **International Date Line** roughly follows line of longitude 180°. When it is crossed, the day changes. Travellers going westwards lose a day, while those going eastwards gain a day. Time zones and the Date Line are bent to follow the boundaries of countries or states to avoid confusion for people living in the areas.

▼ 10.9 Time zones

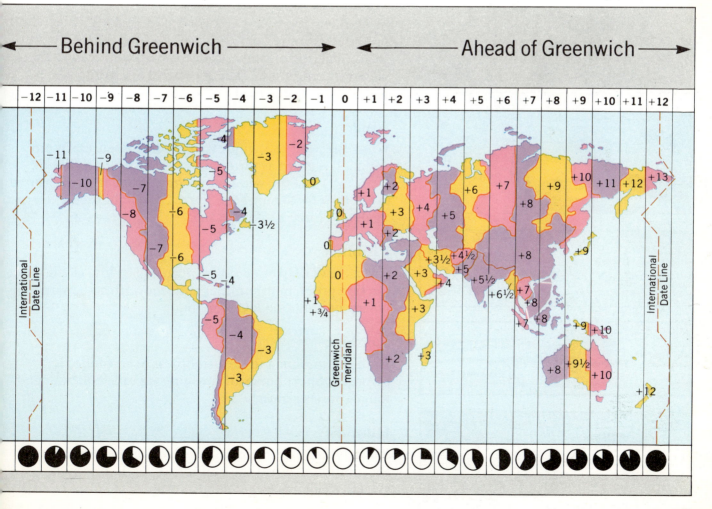

47

11   Will it rain today?

Weather has an important effect on our lives. The success of a holiday may depend on it. Choice of clothes and even some of our moods are linked to it. Weather and **climate** are not the same. Climate is the average weather conditions over many years. It is what we should get at each season. Weather is what arrives on the day! Weather ingredients are explained below.

Rainfall

Rainfall is one form of **precipitation**. Others are snow, sleet and hail. The amount of precipitation each year and when it falls during the year (the *seasonal distribution*) are important. The intensity of rainfall varies from a fine drizzle to large drops such as occur in thunderstorms.

Temperature

Ground temperature is recorded at the earth's surface, and air temperature 112 cm above it. The highest temperature during a period of time is called the maximum, and the lowest the minimum. The **temperature range** is the difference between the two.

Wind

Wind direction and wind strength are measured. Wind direction is given as the compass direction (east, south, west, etc.) that the wind blows *from*. Strength is measured in knots or force numbers. Force 2 is a light breeze, force 8 a gale and force 12 a hurricane.

Visibility

Clear views may be spoilt by mist, fog or low cloud. Haze can be a problem in summer and smog affects some towns where air pollution levels are high.

Sunshine

Both the amount and the brightness of sunshine are recorded. Short bursts of sunshine are called *intervals* and longer bursts *periods*.

Humidity

Air may feel damp or dry. The damper the air the higher the humidity. When the humidity is high, things like washing will dry less well.

High and low

Air pressure cannot be felt or seen but it is an important part of weather. It is measured by a *barometer* which records the weight of air above a point on the earth's surface. Air pressure is measured in millibars. Places of equal pressure plotted on maps are joined up with lines called **isobars** (see 11.6). Pressure varies with time, and from place to place. 11.1 shows two ways in which air pressure differences occur. Pressure differences cause winds, which blow from high to low pressure (11.1b). The greater the pressure difference, the stronger the wind speed. Because of the earth's rotation and surface friction, winds do not blow straight across the isobars. They blow around areas of low pressure (**cyclones**) in an anticlockwise direction (11.6) and around areas of high pressure (**anticyclones**) in a clockwise direction.

Low pressure, where air is rising as in column B of 11.1b, often brings wet and stormy weather. When air is sinking as in column A, hot sunny conditions occur in summer and cold frosty weather is common in winter.

Why it rains

If damp air (containing a lot of water vapour) is forced to rise, it may form rain. 11.2 shows that, as air rises, it cools and can hold less and less vapour. **Condensation** occurs at the **dew point** temperature when water droplets form. These are seen as cloud. If the air continues to rise, the droplets collide to form drops which fall to earth as rain.

11.3 shows one way that moist air is forced to rise: when it meets a range of hills or mountains. This causes a zone of cloud and rain over the top of the mountains. Rain caused in this way is called **relief rainfall**. As the air falls again on the sheltered (lee) side of the

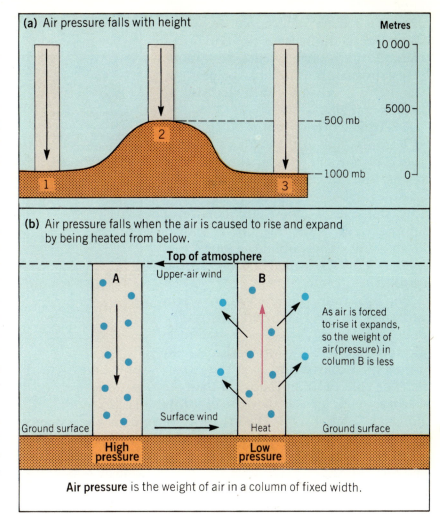

▲ 11.1 Two ways of causing high and low pressure

11.2 Condensation of twenty units of water vapour

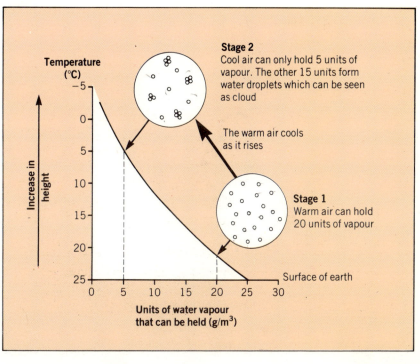

mountain barrier, it gets warmer. The clouds break up because the remaining water droplets change back to vapour by **evaporation**. The area behind the mountains is called the **rain shadow**. It has less rainfall.

A second cause of rain is when damp air becomes hot. If the earth's surface is heated by the sun, it heats the air above it. As the air is heated it expands, becomes lighter and rises. 11.4a shows how this causes cloud and rain on a summer day when the air is moist. 11.4b shows the cumulus clouds that result. This is called **convectional rainfall**.

The final cause of rain is where warm and cold air meet (**frontal rain**). The inset map in 11.5 shows a common meeting place of warm and cold air (called the **polar front**) over the Atlantic. The cold polar air is heavier than the warm tropical air and they usually flow alongside each other. Disturbances in the upper air can cause the lighter warm air to rise over the cold air giving cloud and rain (11.5).

Many disturbances die out but some grow further forming rain-bearing systems called **depressions**. Stages 1–3 in 11.6 show this development as a depression moves eastwards at up to 500 km per day. The anticlockwise swirl of air around the depression centre (low

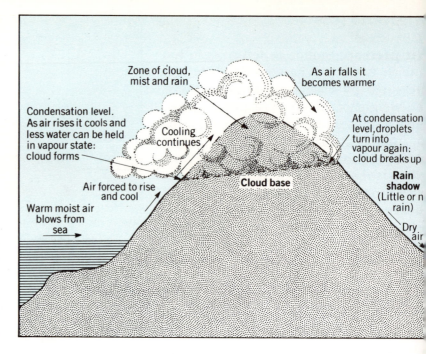

pressure) is clearly shown by the isobar pattern in stage 2 (see also photograph 11.16).

As the system moves eastwards the **cold front** moves faster than the **warm front** and catches it up. The **warm sector** gets gradually smaller (first near the centre of the low) and disappears. There is then no supply of warm moist air left to form more cloud and rain. Once this happens the depression begins to die and pressure stops falling.

Depressions do not simply bring cloud and rain, as the section diagram

▲ **11.3** Formation of relief rainfall

◀ **11.4a** Formation of convectional rainfall

▼ **11.4b** Cumulus clouds

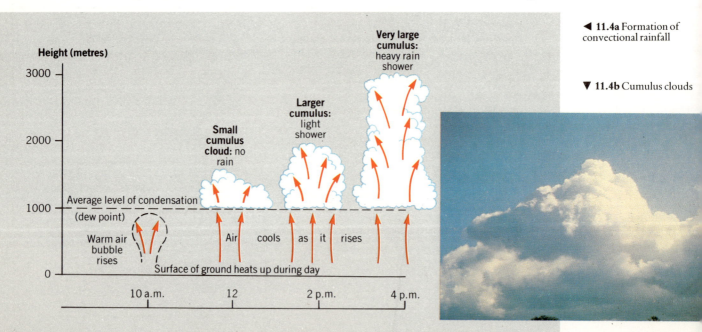

A–B in 11.6 shows. Each part of the depression has characteristics of rain, temperature and wind as described under the section diagram. As the warm front passes over, changes are gradual. The passage of the cold front is, however, often sudden, bringing heavy rain, squally winds and a rapid fall in temperature, followed by a rapid clearance of cloud. Barometer behaviour is a good guide to the possible arrival of a depression. Air pressure falls for 12–48 hours before the first high cirrus clouds are seen ahead of the warm front. A depression can pass in 12 hours but some of the larger slow-moving ones take several days to clear. Depressions often occur in groups, bringing a week or more of unsettled weather.

11.6 A developing depression

► **11.5** Formation of frontal rain over the North Atlantic

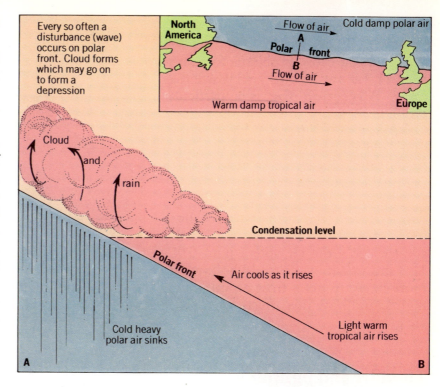

Every so often a disturbance (wave) occurs on polar front. Cloud forms which may go on to form a depression

Cloud and rain

North America

Flow of air
Polar front
A
B
Flow of air

Cold damp polar air

Warm damp tropical air

Europe

Condensation level

Polar front

Air cools as it rises

Light warm tropical air rises

Cold heavy polar air sinks

A

B

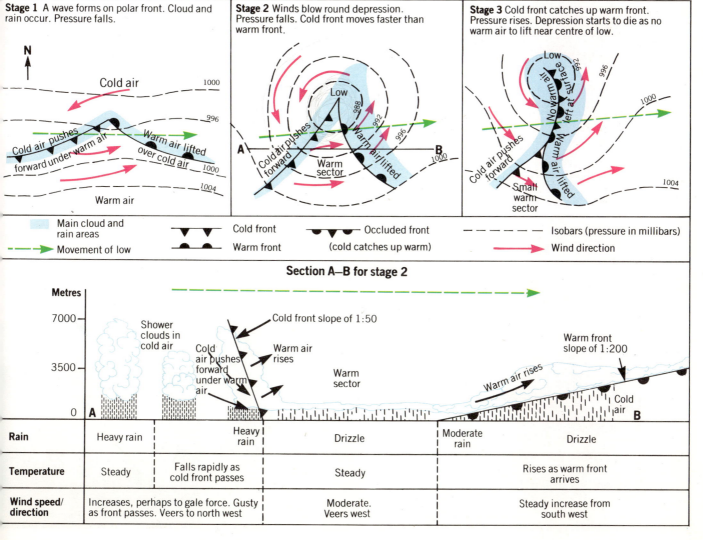

Stage 1 A wave forms on polar front. Cloud and rain occur. Pressure falls.

N

Cold air
1000
996
Cold air pushes forward under warm air
Warm air lifted over cold air
1000
1004
Warm air

Stage 2 Winds blow round depression. Pressure falls. Cold front moves faster than warm front.

Low
988
992
996
1000
A
Cold air pushes forward
Warm air lifted
Warm sector
B

Stage 3 Cold front catches up warm front. Pressure rises. Depression starts to die as no warm air to lift near centre of low.

Low
992
996
No warm air left at surface
Warm air lifted
1000
Cold air pushes forward
Small warm sector
1004

▨ Main cloud and rain areas	▼▼ Cold front	⬤⬤ Occluded front (cold catches up warm)
⟶ Movement of low	⬤⬤ Warm front	--- Isobars (pressure in millibars)
		⟶ Wind direction

Section A–B for stage 2

Metres

7000

3500

0

Shower clouds in cold air

Cold front slope of 1:50

Cold air pushes forward under warm air

Warm air rises

Warm sector

Warm air rises

Warm front slope of 1:200

Cold air

A

B

Rain	Heavy rain	Heavy rain	Drizzle	Moderate rain	Drizzle
Temperature	Steady	Falls rapidly as cold front passes	Steady		Rises as warm front arrives
Wind speed/ direction	Increases, perhaps to gale force. Gusty as front passes. Veers to north west		Moderate. Veers west		Steady increase from south west

Fog and frost

Mist and fog cause problems for transport. 11.7 shows two ways in which fogs form. **Advection fog** is a particular problem as many towns are in valleys. Condensation is increased by air pollution, and smog (smoke and fog) may result. Smokeless zones have done much to ease this problem in British towns.

A ground frost occurs when the temperature of the earth's surface falls to 0 °C. Air frost is when the earth's surface cools the air above it to 0 °C. 11.8 shows why valleys and hollows are more likely to get a frost on calm clear nights, and how this affects what crops are grown.

Thunder and lightning

Thundercloud formation is shown in 11.9a. Lightning (11.9b) is caused by electrical charge differences within the cloud, or between the cloud and earth. This makes air expand violently causing thunder. The intense cold (−20 °C) of the thundercloud shatters hailstones: the positively charged shell splinters are carried upwards and the heavier negatively charged ones move downwards.

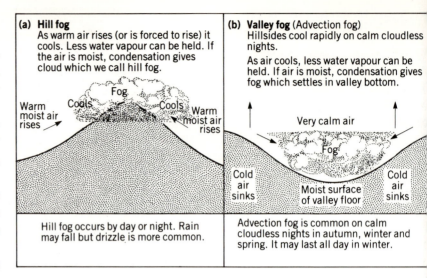

(a) Hill fog
As warm air rises (or is forced to rise) it cools. Less water vapour can be held. If the air is moist, condensation gives cloud which we call hill fog.

Warm moist air rises → Cools — Fog — Cools ← Warm moist air rises

Hill fog occurs by day or night. Rain may fall but drizzle is more common.

(b) Valley fog (Advection fog)
Hillsides cool rapidly on calm cloudless nights.

As air cools, less water vapour can be held. If air is moist, condensation gives fog which settles in valley bottom.

Very calm air — Fog — Cold air sinks — Moist surface of valley floor — Cold air sinks

Advection fog is common on calm cloudless nights in autumn, winter and spring. It may last all day in winter.

▲ **11.7** Hill and valley fog

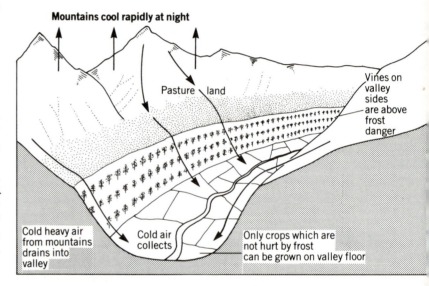

Mountains cool rapidly at night

Pasture land

Vines on valley sides are above frost danger

Cold heavy air from mountains drains into valley

Cold air collects

Only crops which are not hurt by frost can be grown on valley floor

▲ **11.8** How frost affects crop types in the Rhône Valley, Switzerland

◄ **11.9a** Thunderstorm development on a hot moist day

▼ **11.9b** Lightning strike

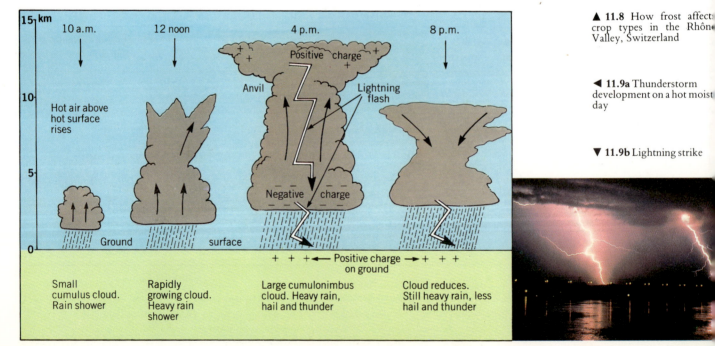

10 a.m.	12 noon	4 p.m.	8 p.m.

Positive charge

Anvil

Lightning flash

Hot air above hot surface rises

Negative charge

Ground surface

← Positive charge → on ground

Small cumulus cloud. Rain shower

Rapidly growing cloud. Heavy rain shower

Large cumulonimbus cloud. Heavy rain, hail and thunder

Cloud reduces. Still heavy rain, less hail and thunder

Disaster

Weather can often be partly to blame for serious accidents. In March 1977 at Tenerife airport in the Canary Isles, the world's worst air disaster took place with a death toll of 574. Two Boeing 747 jumbo jets collided on the runway in thick mist (11.10).

Motorway pile-ups in fog are common, despite warning signals. 200 vehicles collided on the M6 in September 1971, killing 11 and injuring 60. The cost of disasters such as these is enormous, not only in insurance claims but also in human suffering.

Supply and demand

Seasonal temperature differences mean that the demand for power for heating our homes and places of work changes. 11.11 shows changes in demand for electricity. A cold frosty morning brings a sudden demand as people switch on fires when they get up. The Central Electricity Generating Board need accurate weather forecasts because electricity cannot be stored and they must be able to supply extra power as soon as the demand arises.

Gale force

Gale force winds (over 64 km/h) are common in Britain and **hurricane** gusts over 160 km/h are recorded in most years. The worst gale to strike Britain was in December 1703 when 8125 people died. Depressions are responsible for these winds. Suspension bridges such as the Severn and Forth are often closed to high-sided vehicles because of gales, and so are exposed sections of motorways. It is at sea that gales cause most problems, however. 11.12 shows a storm-bound North Sea oil platform. The platforms are designed to withstand a freak wave of 30 metres height. Supply boats can only operate with waves below 2 metres but, for 90% of the winter months, waves are higher.

▲ 11.10 Tenerife air disaster

▼ 11.11 Variation in seasonal demand for electricity

(Graph: Demand (thousands of megawatts) vs Time of day. Curves labelled "Typical winter day" and "Typical summer day".)

▼ 11.12 North Sea oil platform

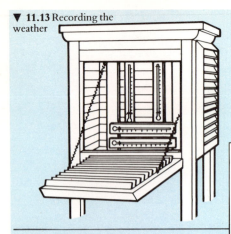

Stevenson screen

Stands 112cm off ground to let air circulate under it. Painted white to reflect heat. Slatted sides to let air circulate. All features designed to allow very accurate measurement of air temperature.

Maximum thermometer

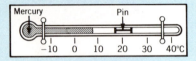

When temperature rises mercury expands and pushes pin up. When temperature falls mercury contracts leaving pin behind. Maximum temperature read from bottom of pin.

Minimum thermometer

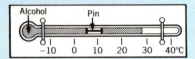

When temperature falls pin is pulled down by alcohol. When temperature rises alcohol expands leaving pin behind. Minimum temperature read from top of pin.

Hygrometer

Measures amount of water vapour in air

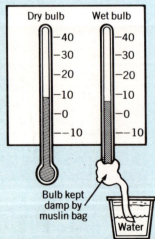

Water is lost from the muslin bag by evaporation. The dryer the air the more water that evaporates. The heat needed for evaporation is taken from bulb. The difference between wet and dry bulb temperature tells us how much water vapour is present: the humidity.

A weather station

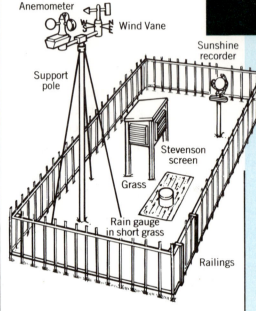

Sited on flat open ground away from trees and buildings.

The **maximum/minimum thermometers** are reset every 24 hours. A new recording card is put in the **sunshine recorder** every 24 hours. The **rain gauge** is emptied every 24 hours.

Anemometer and wind vane

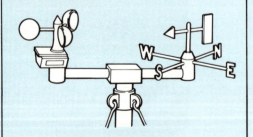

Both are mounted on a pole 10m high.

The cups of the **anemometer** spin round. They are connected to a revolution counter. The number of revolutions in a given time gives the wind speed.

The **wind vane** gives wind direction by pointing *into* the wind. Wind direction is always stated as where it blows from.

Sunshine recorder

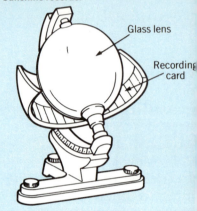

When sun shines the lens scorches a brown line on recording card.

Section of recording card

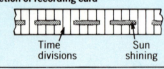

Rain gauge

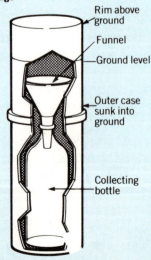

The rim stops water splashing in.

The water in the bottle is poured into a measuring cylinder which gives rainfall in millimetres.

Recording the weather

Getting an accurate picture of what the weather has been like is vital when forecasting future weather. 11.13 shows the range of equipment found at weather stations, and a weather satellite which sends back pictures from space. The weather station also keeps a continual record of air pressure using a **barograph** where an inked pen is attached to a barometer and records changes on graph paper covering a revolving drum.

Getting it right

11.14 shows how all the information collected is used to make a forecast. All countries freely exchange weather information allowing a complete picture to be built up. Satellites provide vital data for oceans and remote land regions such as Antarctica. Long-range forecasts rely on studying records to match present weather conditions with similar conditions in the past, to see what kind of weather is likely to follow.

11.15 shows the weather map and 11.16 the corresponding satellite photograph of a depression north of Britain. The warm and cold fronts on the map are linked to the depression. Weather maps are drawn every 6 hours and, by looking back over several, the rate of movement of weather systems can be worked out. The depression and fronts in 11.15 and 11.16 are moving eastwards at 25 km/h. The likely weather changes expected in the next 24 hours can then be forecast.

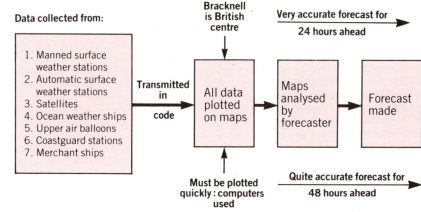

Data collected from:

1. Manned surface weather stations
2. Automatic surface weather stations
3. Satellites
4. Ocean weather ships
5. Upper air balloons
6. Coastguard stations
7. Merchant ships

Transmitted in code → All data plotted on maps

Bracknell is British centre → Maps analysed by forecaster → Forecast made

Very accurate forecast for 24 hours ahead

Must be plotted quickly: computers used

Quite accurate forecast for 48 hours ahead

▲ **11.14** How a weather forecast is made

▼ **11.15** A weather map and symbols

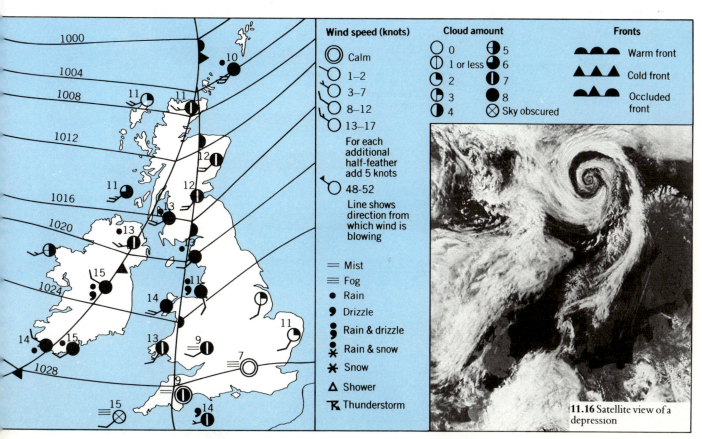

11.16 Satellite view of a depression

12 Global models

Life from the sun

Without light and heat from the sun there would be no life on earth. 12.1a shows that only half of the incoming **energy** reaches the earth's surface. The rest is taken up by the atmosphere or reflected into space. 12.1b shows what happens to the energy received.

The amount of energy received at different **latitudes** varies because of the curvature of the earth and the angle of the sun. In 12.2a the effect of the curvature of the earth can be clearly seen. The further from the **equator** the greater the amount of the earth's surface and atmosphere that must be heated. Each square kilometre near the poles therefore receives much less heat than the same area on the equator. The changing angles of the mid-day sun at

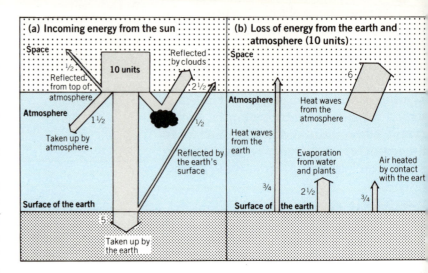

▲ **12.1** Heat in and out (all units are approximate)

different latitudes are shown in 12.2b. The earth's surface receives most heat when the sun's angle is 90° (directly above). At smaller angles, the sunlight has to travel through more of the atmosphere.

▼ **12.2** Angle of sun

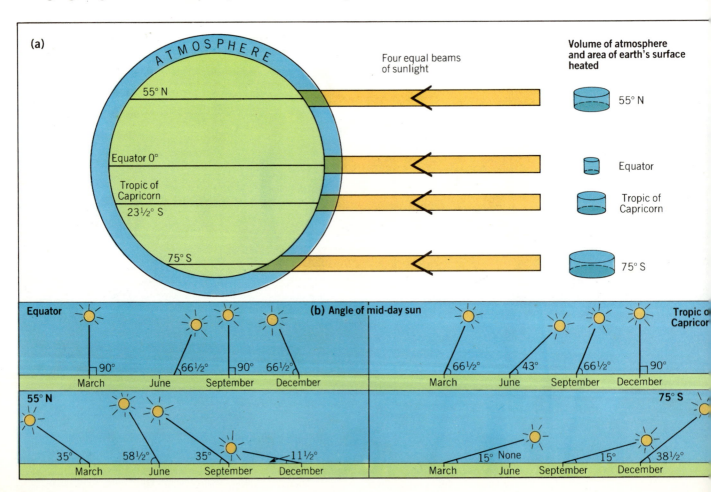

The heat cycle

Areas near the equator are gaining heat from the sun all the time. Those near the poles lose more heat than the sun provides (see 12.3). Yet equatorial areas are not getting hotter and polar areas are not getting colder. This is because heat from around the equator moves outwards to warm other areas. It is this movement of heat energy which produces the main pattern of the world's **climate.**

Around the equator, where heating by the sun is greatest, air rises. This sets in motion the cycle of air movement shown in 12.4.

Air from equatorial areas moves north and south at great height, sinking to produce the **sub-tropical high-pressure zones**. Surface winds move outwards from these areas. At about 60°

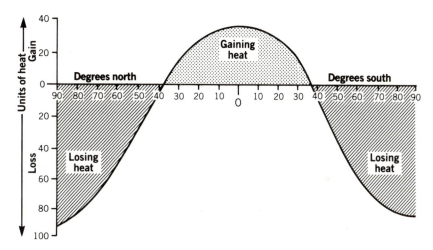

▲ **12.3** Heat loss and gain

north and south the air is again forced upwards as it meets cold polar air. It moves north and south at great height. At the poles the now very cold air sinks to form **polar high pressure**, so completing the cycle.

▼ **12.4** A simple model of air movement

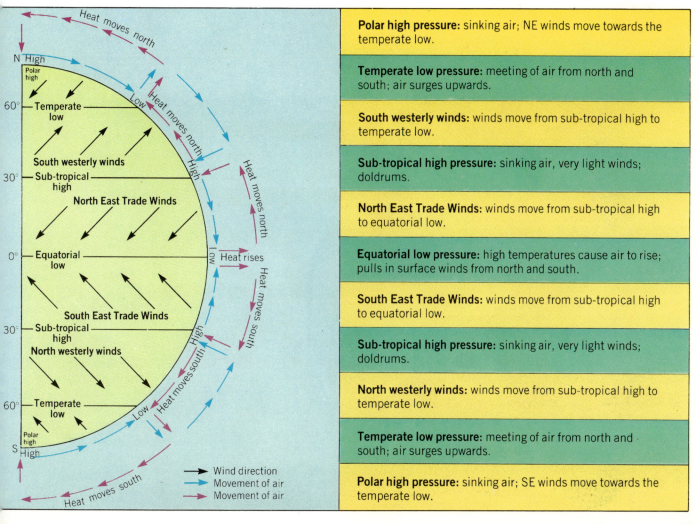

Polar high pressure: sinking air; NE winds move towards the temperate low.

Temperate low pressure: meeting of air from north and south; air surges upwards.

South westerly winds: winds move from sub-tropical high to temperate low.

Sub-tropical high pressure: sinking air, very light winds; doldrums.

North East Trade Winds: winds move from sub-tropical high to equatorial low.

Equatorial low pressure: high temperatures cause air to rise; pulls in surface winds from north and south.

South East Trade Winds: winds move from sub-tropical high to equatorial low.

Sub-tropical high pressure: sinking air, very light winds; doldrums.

North westerly winds: winds move from sub-tropical high to temperate low.

Temperate low pressure: meeting of air from north and south; air surges upwards.

Polar high pressure: sinking air; SE winds move towards the temperate low.

Seasons come and seasons go

With the changing seasons the overhead mid-day sun moves north and south. This means that the zone of maximum heating, and the **equatorial low pressure**, also move. All other **climate** zones are therefore moved (see 12.5). This is why some areas of the world have different pressure and wind conditions, and therefore different weather, at different times of the year.

The general pattern of world climatic zones is complicated in a number of ways. The oceans are particularly important since, as 12.6 shows, water is constantly moving around. When water moves away from the equator, it forms warm currents, which warm the land masses they flow around. When water moves towards the equator it forms cold currents, cooling coastal areas.

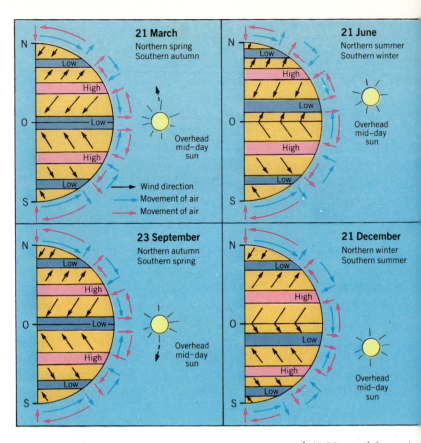

▼ **12.6** Ocean currents

▲ **12.5** Seasonal changes in pressure

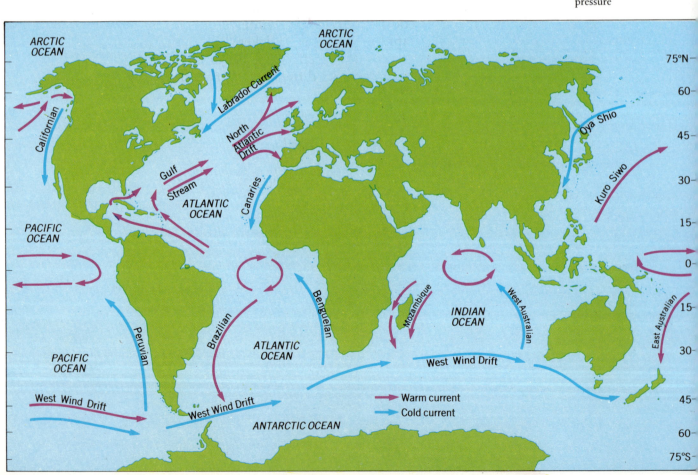

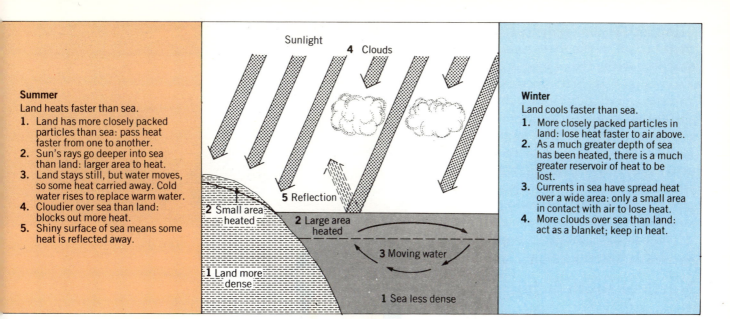

Summer
Land heats faster than sea.

1. Land has more closely packed particles than sea: pass heat faster from one to another.
2. Sun's rays go deeper into sea than land: larger area to heat.
3. Land stays still, but water moves, so some heat carried away. Cold water rises to replace warm water.
4. Cloudier over sea than land: blocks out more heat.
5. Shiny surface of sea means some heat is reflected away.

Sunlight
4 Clouds
5 Reflection
2 Small area heated
2 Large area heated
3 Moving water
1 Land more dense
1 Sea less dense

Winter
Land cools faster than sea.

1. More closely packed particles in land: lose heat faster to air above.
2. As a much greater depth of sea has been heated, there is a much greater reservoir of heat to be lost.
3. Currents in sea have spread heat over a wide area: only a small area in contact with air to lose heat.
4. More clouds over sea than land: act as a blanket; keep in heat.

The **North Atlantic Drift** acts like a hot-water bottle around Britain in winter, keeping temperatures up to 20 °C warmer than some areas at similar latitudes. The **Californian Current** chills cities such as San Francisco, giving them cool summers, and frequent fogs as cold sea air meets the warm land.

Maritime or continental

Nearness to the sea or even large lakes also has an important effect on the climate. Areas which are especially affected by the sea are called **maritime**, while those far inland are called **continental**. The effect of the sea is greatest when winds regularly blow inland (onshore winds). Where there are usually offshore winds, the sea has less effect. Maritime areas have a much smaller **temperature range** than continental areas. Summers are cooler and winters

milder than the average for the latitude. Continental areas have extreme temperatures, with warmer summers and colder winters than the average for the latitude.

12.7 is a summary of the major reasons for these differences, showing why land heats up in the summer and cools down in the winter much more rapidly than seas or lakes. 12.8 shows the combined effects of ocean currents and land/sea differences between 40° and 60° north.

Higher and higher

It was shown earlier that temperature decreases with height in the atmosphere, and that high land can produce **relief rainfall**. This means that mountainous areas have very different climates than nearby lowland areas. Usually they are colder and wetter.

▲ **12.7** Land and sea differences

▼ **12.8** A temperature transect

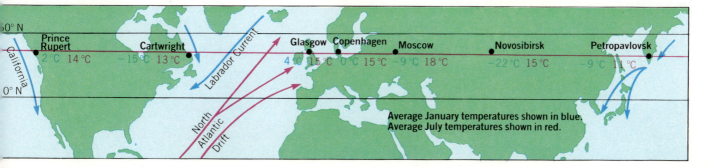

60° N
Prince Rupert 2 °C 14 °C
Cartwright −15 °C 13 °C
California
Labrador Current
North Atlantic Drift
Glasgow 4 °C 15 °C
Copenhagen 0 °C 15 °C
Moscow −9 °C 18 °C
Novosibirsk −22 °C 15 °C
Petropavlovsk −9 °C 11 °C
40° N
Average January temperatures shown in blue.
Average July temperatures shown in red.

In 12.9a the **tropical grassland vegetation** in the foreground contrasts sharply with the summit of Mount Kilimanjaro at 5895 metres, which is snow covered all year. 12.9b shows the different vegetation zones on this mountain. Above 4500 metres there is snow for at least part of the year, and only the most hardy plants, usually found at low levels around 60° north and south, can survive. Moving down-slope, plants become gradually less hardy, until the grassland typical of the latitude is reached.

North or south facing?

Where valleys run east to west through mountainous areas, the valleys sides have very different climates. In 12.10 the left hand northern side (which faces south) gets more sunlight and is therefore much warmer and better for farming. The right hand southern side (which faces north) is nearly always in shadow. The direction in which a place faces is called its **aspect**.

Ever changing

Climate maps are based on average figures recorded over many years. However, few years are ever like the average, and seasons are sometimes very different from expected. 12.11 shows a scene during a particularly cold British winter in 1684. In contrast, the summers of 1975 and 1976 were much drier and warmer than usual in Britain.

12.9a Mount Kilimanjaro

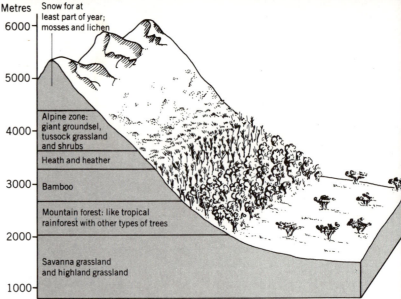

▲ **12.9b** Vegetation changes on Mount Kilimanjaro

◄ **12.10** Aspect

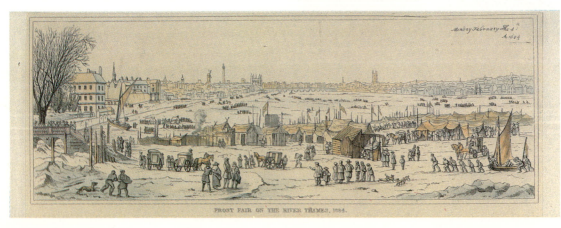

FROST FAIR ON THE RIVER THAMES, 1684.

◄ **12.11** The frozen Thames

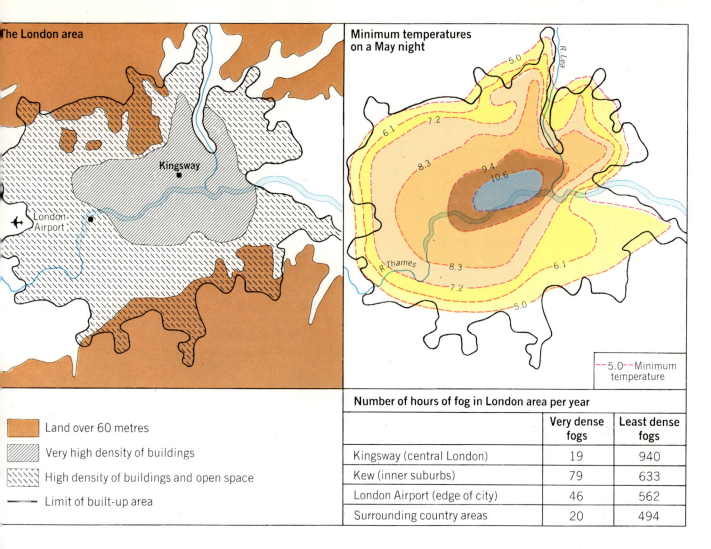

The London area

Minimum temperatures on a May night

- 5.0 - - Minimum temperature

Land over 60 metres

Very high density of buildings

High density of buildings and open space

Limit of built-up area

Number of hours of fog in London area per year		
	Very dense fogs	Least dense fogs
Kingsway (central London)	19	940
Kew (inner suburbs)	79	633
London Airport (edge of city)	46	562
Surrounding country areas	20	494

▲ 12.12 London's micro-climate

▼ 12.13 The effects of urban areas on climate

Urban climates

People can change the **local** or **micro-climate** in many ways. The most dramatic of these is the building of towns and cities.

12.12 shows some of the effects of the large built-up area of Greater London on the micro-climate. The steady increase in temperature towards the centre can be clearly seen. The area in the north along the River Lea, and to the east along the Thames, shows how even small areas of open land can lead to lower temperatures. The increase in the number of fogs can also be seen.

While each urban area produces a different micro-climate, it is possible to see similarities between them all. 12.13 is a summary of the main effects seen in towns and cities throughout the world.

Temperature	Usually higher than rural areas: most noticeable when little wind. Much heat given out by buildings: keeps nights warmer. Heat is lost more slowly at night, but also builds up more slowly in mornings. Open spaces within the urban area warm up most, because they are sheltered by buildings.
Precipitation	Difficult to tell. Pollution may cause more vapour to condense. More summer thunderstorms. Snow in rural areas becomes rain or sleet in city. Snow melts more quickly.
Wind	Usually less windy because buildings act like windbreaks. More calm days, but also more very strong winds because of wind being forced between high-sided buildings.
Visibility	Pollution from chimneys and exhausts causes poorer visibility, especially if urban area is in a valley, and in calm conditions. More fogs/smogs. Fogs last longer. Cloudier.
Sunshine	Less sunshine and more cloudy. More hazy and weak sunshine because of pollution blocking out some light. Tall buildings make large shadows.
Humidity	Lower than in rural areas. Little vegetation or water on surface of ground.

Sorting it out

12.14 shows the climate regions that could be expected based on the model shown in 12.4 and 12.5. However, it should now be clear that many other factors can alter this pattern. 12.15 shows the actual position of climatic types.

In later chapters the links between these **climate zones** and vegetation will be explored. 12.16 shows that in many parts of the world climate and **natural vegetation zones** are very similar, but that elsewhere differences do occur. It must also be remembered that in many parts of the world the natural vegetation has been completely cleared to make room for towns, farmland or commercial forests.

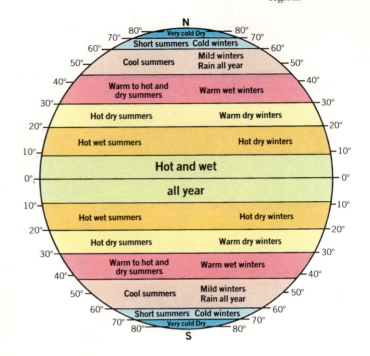

▼ **12.14** A model of climate regions

▼ **12.15** World climate types

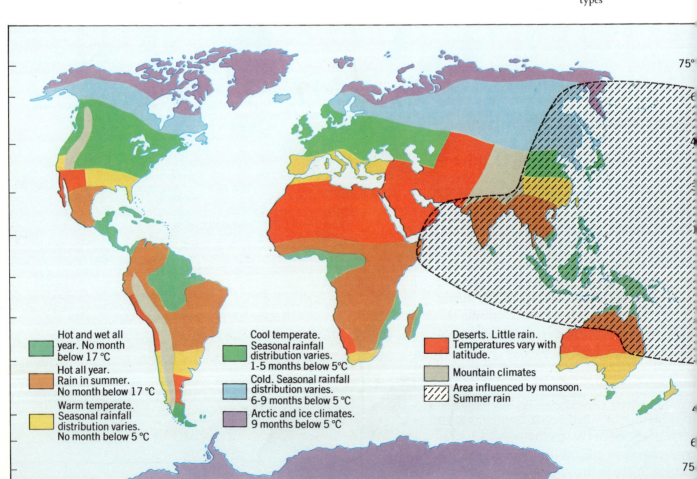

Hot and wet all year. No month below 17 °C

Hot all year. Rain in summer. No month below 17 °C

Warm temperate. Seasonal rainfall distribution varies. No month below 5 °C

Cool temperate. Seasonal rainfall distribution varies. 1–5 months below 5°C

Cold. Seasonal rainfall distribution varies. 6–9 months below 5 °C

Arctic and ice climates. 9 months below 5 °C

Deserts. Little rain. Temperatures vary with latitude.

Mountain climates

Area influenced by monsoon. Summer rain

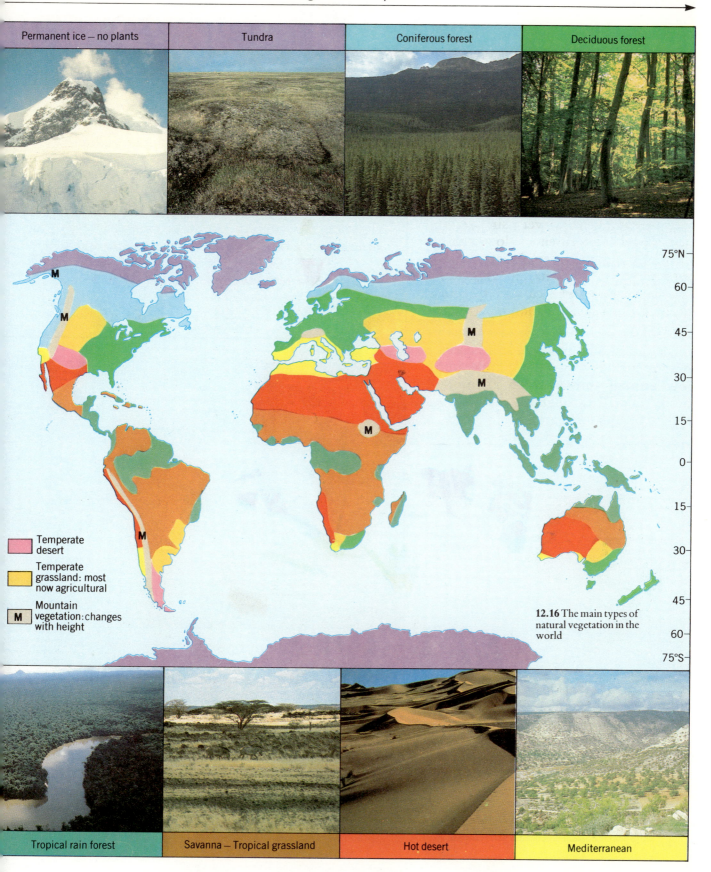

Permanent ice – no plants

Tundra

Coniferous forest

Deciduous forest

75°N
60
45
30
15
0
15
30
45
60
75°S

Temperate desert

Temperate grassland: most now agricultural

M Mountain vegetation: changes with height

12.16 The main types of natural vegetation in the world

Tropical rain forest

Savanna – Tropical grassland

Hot desert

Mediterranean

13.1 describes conditions in the Amazon basin where the climate is hot and wet. 13.2 shows the areas which have this type of **equatorial climate**. They are low lying and mostly within 10° of the equator. The mid-day sun is always high in the sky. Day and night are of roughly equal length throughout the year. The heat causes air to rise and **convectional** thunderclouds form (see page 50). This rising air draws in the **Trade Winds** (see page 57).

The air contains a lot of water vapour (has a high humidity) and feels sticky and unpleasant. 13.3 shows temperatures (line graph) and rainfall (columns) for Singapore. 13.4 suggests what information should be taken from climate graphs such as this. High temperature, low **annual temperature range** and heavy rainfall throughout the year are typical of equatorial areas.

The heat increases rapidly towards two o'clock. The leaves which were so moist and fresh in the early morning are now tired and drooping. The eastern horizon becomes suddenly black, then wind rushes through the forest, a vivid flash of lightning, a crash of thunder and finally the downpour of rain. All nature is refreshed. The next day the sun rises in a cloudless sky and the cycle is completed – spring summer autumn as it were in one tropical day.

Adapted from **H.W. Bates,** *The Naturalist on the River Amazon*

▲ 13.1

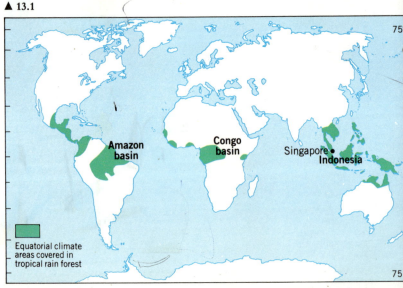

▲ **13.2** Equatorial climate regions

Equatorial climate areas covered in tropical rain forest

▼ **13.3** The climate of Singapore

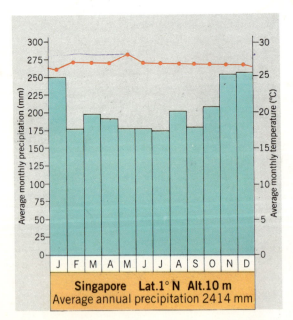

Singapore   Lat.1°N Alt.10 m
Average annual precipitation 2414 mm

▼ **13.4** Climate terms

To get the most out of a climate graph the following should always be worked out

To do with temperature

1. **The maximum annual temperature** The highest monthly temperature of the year. What is it (in °C) and when does it occur?

2. **The minimum annual temperature** The lowest monthly temperature of the year. What is it (in °C) and when does it occur?

3. **The annual temperature range** The difference (in °C) between 1 and 2 above.

To do with rainfall

1. **The annual rainfall** The total rainfall for the whole year. It is found by adding together all the monthly figures. Measured in millimetres.

2. **The rainfall distribution** Which time(s) of the year is wettest and which is the driest. Described in terms of months and seasons.

So many plants

The **natural vegetation** of equatorial climate areas is **tropical rain forest**. 13.5 shows a view of the forest and 13.6 shows a small section. Plants grow rapidly throughout the year in the ideal 'hot house' conditions. There is great variety of plants: over 40 000 flowering plants in the Amazon lowland and 300 kinds of tree in an area of 2 km². Along river banks, dense jungle undergrowth is found because light reaches the

◀ **13.5** The rain forest

▼ **13.6** A section of equatorial rain forest

Metres		
45	**Upper layer**	Evergreen forest giants
40		
35	Tops of tallest trees	
30		Strangler (parasite)
25	**Middle layer**	Liana (root in soil)
20		Closed canopy
15	Trunks of tallest trees and younger trees	Epiphyte
10		Tall straight trunks
5	**Ground layer**	Young trees fight for light
0	dark and damp	Little undergrowth mainly ferns
		Buttress roots
		Leaf debris
		Shallow roots

◀ **13.7** Adaptations of trees in tropical rain forests

ground. Elsewhere the forest **canopy** cuts out most light and the floor is covered with dead leaves. **Epiphytes** (plants which grow on trees but do not harm them), **parasites** (plants which grow on trees and weaken or kill them) and **lianas** (creepers which use tree trunks for support) are common.

Plants have certain features which let them make the most of the climate in which they grow naturally. These features are called **adaptations** and those found in the rain forest are shown in 13.7.

Adaptation	Reason for adaptation
Evergreen leaves	To allow growth all year round because there is no cold season.
Large leaves	To allow rapid growth in ideal climatic conditions.
Smooth leaves, often pointed (drip tips)	To shed water quickly: plants cannot grow when covered in water.
Thin bark	No need for protection against climate problems.
Buttress roots	To support trees as root system is shallow.
No one season for flowering or fruiting	Climate is similar all year so each tree has its own time for flowering and fruiting.

Clearing the forest

Rain forests occur in developing countries and provide **hardwoods** such as teak and mahogany for sale, mostly to developed countries. Different kinds of tree grow together (**mixed stands**) which makes lumbering difficult. Areas are mapped to see what trees are present, and the different types of wood are separated for sale. Many forests are remote so access roads have to be built (13.8). Sometimes a labour supply must be brought in. Roads often link to river banks from where logs are floated to sawmills nearer the coast ready for export. Few tarmaced roads exist and the heavy rains make movement slow.

Sometimes the cleared areas are replanted with one type of tree for commercial use (**a plantation**). In Malaysia rubber is grown for its sap (latex) which is then sold (13.9). Sometimes the land is cleared for farmland. But little forest is replanted with the same kinds of trees as were chopped down.

Road building, new settlements, mining and factory operation all take their toll on the rain forest (13.10). High population growth is common and, as countries struggle with this problem, rapid forest clearance results. Raw materials such as timber must be sold for cash, and the people fed and housed. Many animals and plants which lived in the forests have become extinct. But an even greater problem is the sudden loss of soil fertility when trees are removed.

◄ **13.8** Lumbering in Malaysia

▼ **13.9** A rubber plantation in Malaysia

▼ **13.10a** Highway, Malaysia

▼ **13.10b** New settlement in Brazil

▼ **13.10c** Opencast copper mine

The key to understanding

Tropical soil is deep and red because of the rapid **chemical weathering** (see unit 4) caused by high temperatures and high rainfall. Any nutrients which cannot be taken up by plant roots are rapidly washed downwards (**leached**). Iron and silica are leached forming a redeposited layer in the **subsoil** (13.11). Trees are vital to the soil as their leaves continually fall to the floor and are rapidly broken down by bacteria. The nutrients released are quickly returned to the tree through the shallow rooting system (13.12). Without trees the soil is no longer fertile. Also the trees break the force of the torrential downpours and their roots bind soil together. Removing forest from even low-angled slopes can lead to very severe **soil erosion** by water.

Traditional farming in rain forests is called 'slash and burn' or **shifting cultivation**. A small patch of trees is cleared to grow crops. The land is farmed for about three years only, while it stays fertile. It is then left for about 30 years to regain its fertility before being used again (13.13).

13.14 shows destruction of a forest for farming in Indonesia. The soil is bare, the land is sloping and water is washing soil downslope. Soon gully erosion may occur (4.8, page 21). There is often a lack of knowledge about soil erosion and a lack of money to do anything about it.

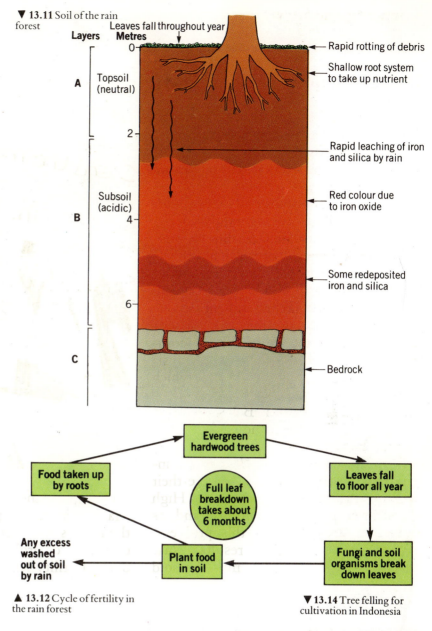

▼ **13.11** Soil of the rain forest

Layers — Metres

Leaves fall throughout year

— Rapid rotting of debris

— Shallow root system to take up nutrient

A — Topsoil (neutral)

— Rapid leaching of iron and silica by rain

— Red colour due to iron oxide

B — Subsoil (acidic)

— Some redeposited iron and silica

C

— Bedrock

Evergreen hardwood trees

Food taken up by roots

Full leaf breakdown takes about 6 months

Leaves fall to floor all year

Any excess washed out of soil by rain

Plant food in soil

Fungi and soil organisms break down leaves

▲ **13.12** Cycle of fertility in the rain forest

▼ **13.14** Tree felling for cultivation in Indonesia

▼ **13.13** Shifting cultivation in the tropical rain forest

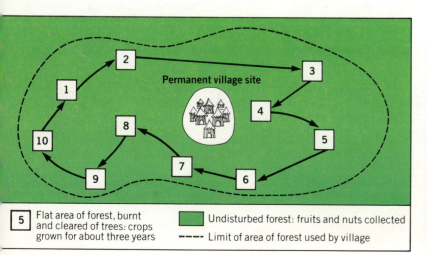

Permanent village site

| 5 | Flat area of forest, burnt and cleared of trees: crops grown for about three years |

Undisturbed forest: fruits and nuts collected

– – – Limit of area of forest used by village

Green or yellow

The scenes in 14.1a, b show the sharp contrasts between the **wet season** (summer) and the **dry season** (winter) in many parts of the tropics. Although the summer conditions are very similar to those found in **equatorial** areas, the winter drought is so severe that it is impossible for lush rain forests to survive. Instead the summer scene is one of rich greens. Tall grasses and other plants grow rapidly to produce seeds before the drought starts. When it does arrive, the scene is dominated by yellows and browns as the **vegetation** dries up or lies dormant until the next wet season.

◀ **14.1a** Savanna summer (wet season)

▶ **14.1b** Savanna winter (dry season)

◀ **14.2a** A transect across the savanna

Forest | Park savanna | Savanna | Semi-desert | Desert

— Decreasing rainfall with increasing distance from equator →
About 1200 km

14.2a shows how there is a steady change in vegetation from the equatorial areas outwards. As rainfall decreases, trees become more scarce and **savanna grassland** dominates. As the desert areas are approached, vegetation becomes even more sparse. The savanna grassland is therefore a *transition* or in-between zone, merging into the areas on either side.

14.2b outlines the main characteristics of savanna vegetation. To survive successfully plants must find ways to overcome the long hot winter drought. They must also be able to withstand the fires which can sweep through large areas. These are caused either naturally or by people.

▼ **14.2b** Savanna vegetation

Trees	Grasses
1. Usually no more than 12 metres high.	1. Vary from 80 cm to 4.5 metres high.
2. Mostly deciduous: trees dormant in dry season.	2. Deciduous: leaves die in dry season and roots remain dormant.
3. Fewer and lower trees further from equator (drier).	3. Height and type varies with rainfall: shorter, more wiry and more spaced out as rainfall decreases.
4. Trees only along water courses in drier areas.	4. Grasses mixed with herbs and other small plants, most of which have roots, tubers or bulbs which are resistant to fire and drought.
5. **Acacia** is flat topped, thorny, with long tap roots (thin very deep central root), and shallow roots that spread out like fan.	5. Roots very long, to search for water.
6. **Baobab** stores water in its thick bark and sponge-like wood.	6. Seed cases have hard shells to resist drought and fire.
7. **Eucalyptus** (Australia) has thick tough fire-resistant bark.	7. Grass leaves have narrow blades to reduce water loss.
	8. Some grasses turn edges of leaf towards sun when very hot to reduce water loss.

Winter high and summer low

The major areas of savanna grassland vegetation are shown in 14.3a and the climate graphs of both a northern and southern hemisphere climatic station are shown in 14.3b and c. Although the climate at the two stations is similar, Cuiba is at higher **altitude**, which both lowers the temperature and increases the rainfall.

In March the overhead mid-day sun crosses the equator and by early summer it is over the northern savanna areas (Kayes) where it stays until late summer (see 12.5). It brings with it the zone of **equatorial low pressure** and the **convectional rainfall** described in units 12 and 11. The increase in cloud cover at this time reduces the temperature slightly, so May is the hottest month. In September the overhead mid-day sun moves into the southern hemisphere, and the **sub-tropical high-pressure zone** steadily moves south to cover the northern hemisphere savanna lands (see 12.4 and 12.5). This zone of sinking air produces clear skies and very dry or even drought conditions. The sun is still high enough in the sky to produce hot days, and night temperatures rarely fall below 15 °C, even in mid-winter.

Soil like a brick

The soils found in the tropical grassland areas, shown in 14.4, are similar in many ways to those of the **tropical rain forest**. High temperatures make dead vegetation break down rapidly, but there is less debris than in the forests, and for half of the year little grows. This makes the **topsoil** thin.

Silica and iron are again **leached** downwards, making a very red soil. The high temperatures lead to much **chemical weathering** of the bedrock so that, especially on flat areas, the **subsoil** becomes very deep. In the dry season, moisture is drawn upwards in the soil, drying it into a very hard brick-like substance, which can be used

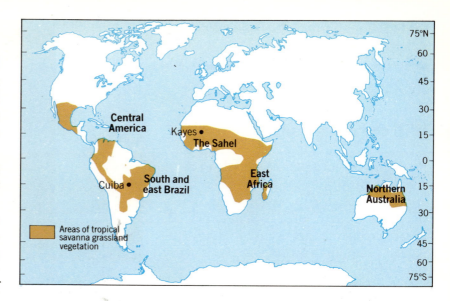

▲ **14.3a** Areas of savanna vegetation

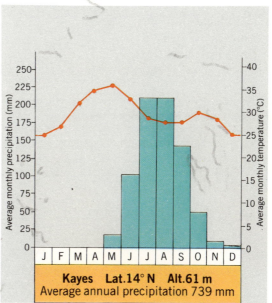

Kayes   Lat.14° N   Alt.61 m
Average annual precipitation 739 mm

◀ **14.3b** The climate of Kayes

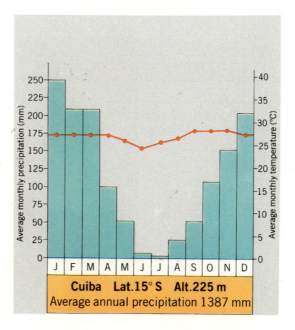

Cuiba   Lat.15° S   Alt.225 m
Average annual precipitation 1387 mm

◀ **14.3c** The climate of Cuiba

for building. This type of soil used to be called a **laterite**. The name is taken from the Latin word 'later' which means a brick.

Will the rains come?

People living in savanna grassland areas rely on summer rains to give them enough water for the whole year. When the rains are late, or less than expected, great problems are caused. Unfortunately, rainfall in these areas is very unreliable.

The northern half of Nigeria is in the Sahel (see 14.3a) and 14.5a and b show that only Jos, on higher land, has had its normal rains since about 1970. 14.5c shows both the recent problems and the great variations from year to year in the

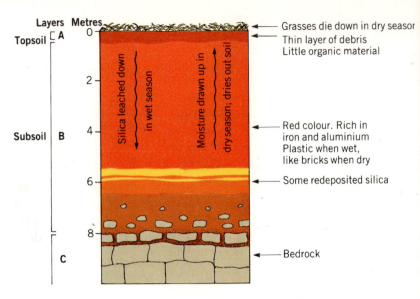

▲ **14.4** Tropical wet/dry soils

Sahel. 14.6 shows how animals can suffer in dry years, and in the worst affected areas people are only kept alive by help from groups such as Oxfam and Save the Children.

Changing climate

Because there has been less rainfall than usual for many years in the Sahel, the Sahara Desert has moved southwards. This may have been caused by a natural movement in the pressure belts, or by people destroying the **natural vegetation**. Fires sometimes occur naturally, but have often been used to clear the grassland for farming. In places goats, sheep and cattle have been allowed to overgraze the land, making it impossible for the vegetation to regrow. This may lead to **soil erosion**.

◄ **14.5** Changing rainfall patterns

▼ **14.6** Savanna drought

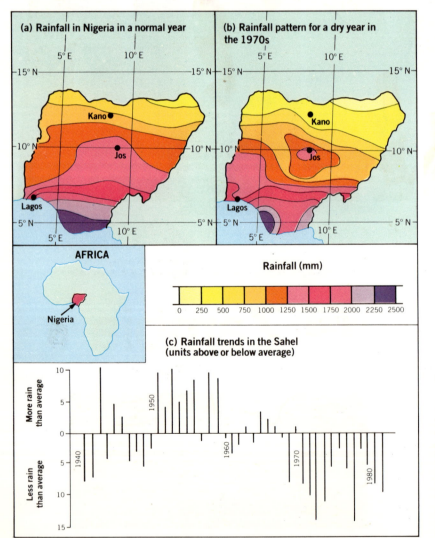

Changing farming

Farming is often primitive in these areas, and in the drier parts scraping a living is always difficult. Traditional farming relies on hard work, and only hand tools are used. Farmers cannot afford machinery or fertilisers, and have little knowledge of modern methods. In some areas attempts have been made to improve farming by using **irrigation**: for example, in Central Nigeria where wheat yields have been improved. In Australian tropical grasslands, large beef-cattle ranches have been very successfully established, often relying on water from bore-holes in the dry season.

The future?

As natural vegetation is destroyed and more land farmed, wildlife is pushed into smaller areas or completely wiped out. Some countries have created parks or reserves to save some natural areas, and increasing numbers of tourists are attracted to them. 14.7 shows an advertisement to attract visitors from Britain to Zambia. The money which tourists spend can be of great benefit in helping the country to develop.

▼ **14.7** Tourism in Zambia

There are few really great experiences left in life that can truly compare with the breathtaking thrill and sheer excitement of a safari holiday in Zambia.

Zambia with the mighty Zambezi River which surges headlong over the spectacular and unforgettable Victoria Falls. A sight which creates such stunning cloud vapours that it is known in Zambia as MOSI-OA TUNYA—THE SMOKE THAT THUNDERS.

Zambia where you can witness the daily drama unfold of roaming lions, majestic elephants, thundering herds of buffalo and zebra; graceful antelope and a thousand and one colourful birds in their natural habitat.

From the very first moment you set foot into one of Zambia's eighteen magnificent National Parks, your holiday experience of a lifetime begins.

Most of the holiday accommodation takes place in self contained lodges which offer all modern facilities. So why not take a walk on the wild side and safari in Zambia where you can come face to face with the real Africa.

For more details on Safari Package holidays to Zambia contact your nearest official tour organiser listed below or fill in coupon.

PACKAGE TOUR ENQUIRIES

One of the world's last great adventures...

Zambia
The big game country!

I would like to experience one of the world's last great adventures. Please forward me details on safari holidays in Zambia.

Name _____

Address _____

_____

To Zambia National Tourist Board, 163 Piccadilly, London W1V 9DE. Tel 01-493 1188/01-493 0848

Large parts of South East Asia and coastal Northern Australia (see 12.15, page 62) have a **monsoon climate**. 15.1 gives information about conditions in India where much of the country has a monsoon climate. These areas have three seasons. The **hot dry season** (March–June) has the highest temperatures just before the monsoon 'breaks'. This brings in the **hot wet season** (June–October) when heavy rainfall with thunder occurs. Cloud and high humidity cause temperatures to fall in the summer months. The **cooler dry season** (October–February) brings much more pleasant conditions.

The cause of the monsoon rains is the seasonal shift of winds over India caused by pressure changes (15.2). In summer the high temperatures cause low pressure to form over India. This draws in warm moist onshore winds from the

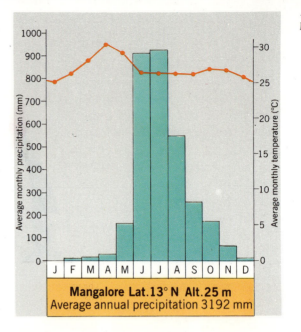

◄ **15.1** The climate of Mangalore

Mangalore Lat.13° N Alt.25 m
Average annual precipitation 3192 mm

ocean to the south which bring cloud and rain. In winter cool dry air causes high pressure over India and gentle offshore winds blow southwards towards low pressure over the ocean (15.3).

▼ **15.2** Seasonal pressure and wind changes in South Asia and Northern Australia

▼ **15.3** Seasonal pressure and wind changes over Ind

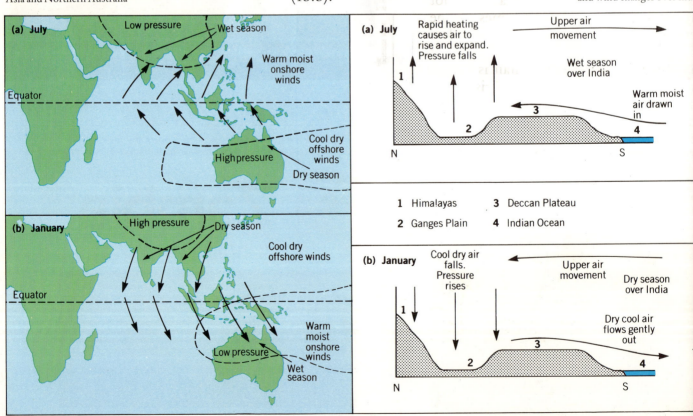

15.4 shows that the start (burst) of the monsoon is some 6–8 weeks earlier in south east India than in north west India. It advances northwards as the warm moist air is drawn ever further inland. At the end of the wet season the rains retreat southwards as pressure rises (caused by shortening days and lower temperatures). The Western Ghat mountains cause much **relief rainfall** (see page 50) as winds are forced to rise. To the east of them a **rain shadow** effect occurs (15.4).

Too much or too little

The monsoon rains are very unreliable. In northern Sri Lanka July rainfall is expected to be 30 mm. But 15.5 shows that, for nearly half of the years in a 40-year period, little or no rain fell in July. The main crop of monsoon Asia is rice. The rice seedlings are grown in watered nursery beds during the hot dry season. They must then be transplanted to paddy fields which rely on monsoon rains to flood them (15.6). Monsoon countries are usually poor and cannot afford costly irrigation schemes. If the crop fails, starvation will follow unless food is provided by organisations such as Oxfam. Too much rainfall is just as serious (15.7). 15.8 summarises the problems caused by the monsoon climate. These put great strains on the economies of countries in South East Asia.

▼ **15.7** Madras shanties after flood

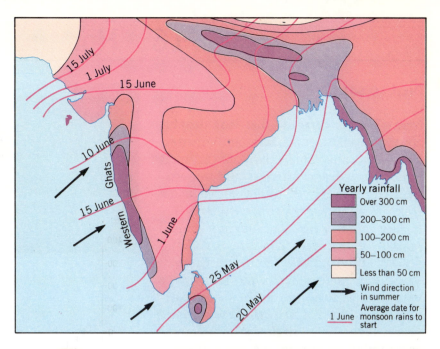

▲ **15.4** The varying effect of the monsoon in India

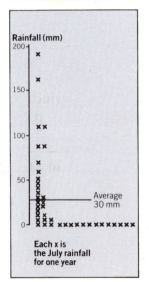

Rainfall (mm)

Each x is the July rainfall for one year

◄ **15.5** Variation in July rainfall in northern Sri Lanka

▲ **15.6** Paddy fields

▼ **15.8** The problems of the monsoon climate

Rest of world

Monsoon Asia

Over 50% of the world's population live in monsoon Asia. Most rely on the monsoon rain for farming. The monsoon is unreliable and causes many problems.

Problems over timing. When the monsoon is late, planting is delayed and crop yields are lower. Water needed for irrigation is not available.

Problems with the amount of rain. When the monsoon fails or little rain falls, famine, starvation and death result. When too much rain falls, the valleys (where most people live) are flooded. Crops and houses are destroyed, seeds are washed out and landslips occur.

Violent storms at the end of the rainy season. These cause problems on the coasts where tidal waves kill many people who live in low-lying areas.
1876 12-metre tidal wave killed 100 000 in Bangladesh.
1971   7-metre tidal wave killed 300 000 in eastern India.

Not so sandy

Many people imagine that **hot deserts** always consist of sand and **dunes**. However, only small parts of the areas which have desert **climate** and **vegetation** are sandy. A much more usual scene is the rocky waste shown in 16.1.

Any area with an average annual rainfall of less than 250 mm is called a desert, and 16.2 shows their locations. Very few places have no rain for a whole year, although in the driest parts of the world it has not rained for tens of years. Average figures for temperature and rainfall give little real idea of what desert weather is like. 16.3a shows the climate of Timbuktu, while 16.3b and c show the great daily or **diurnal range** of temperature. The cloudless skies allow the sun to heat up the ground rapidly, and temperatures may reach 75 °C. At night heat escapes rapidly into the atmosphere, and frosts have been known.

16.4 shows how **sub-tropical high pressure** leads to hot deserts being formed. Cold ocean currents off the western coasts of desert areas can also play a part.

◄ **16.1** Rocky desert

▼ **16.2** Areas of desert vegetation

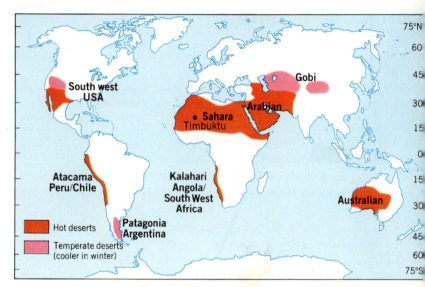

Hot deserts

Temperate deserts (cooler in winter)

▼ **16.3a** The climate of Timbuktu

▼ **16.3b,c** Diurnal temperature changes at Timbuktu

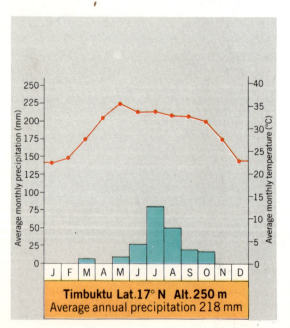

Timbuktu Lat.17° N Alt.250 m
Average annual precipitation 218 mm

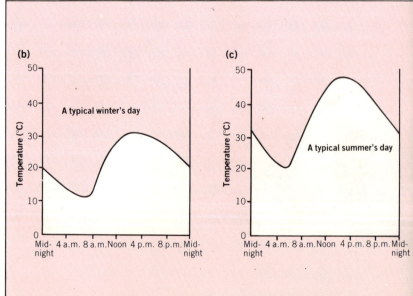

(b) A typical winter's day

(c) A typical summer's day

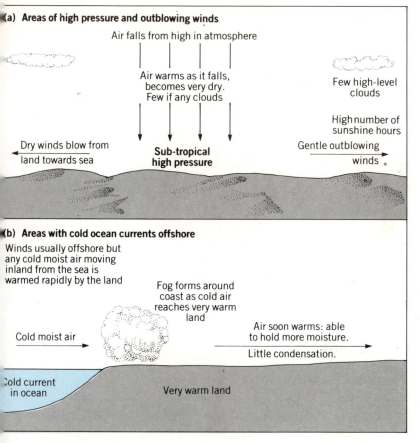

(a) Areas of high pressure and outblowing winds

Air falls from high in atmosphere

Air warms as it falls, becomes very dry. Few if any clouds

Few high-level clouds

High number of sunshine hours

Dry winds blow from land towards sea

Sub-tropical high pressure

Gentle outblowing winds

(b) Areas with cold ocean currents offshore

Winds usually offshore but any cold moist air moving inland from the sea is warmed rapidly by the land

Fog forms around coast as cold air reaches very warm land

Air soon warms: able to hold more moisture. Little condensation.

Cold moist air

Cold current in ocean

Very warm land

16.4 Causes of hot desert

16.5 Rainfall patterns in Abu Dhabi

Year / Month	Year 1 Number of rainy days	Year 1 Rainfall (mm)	Year 2 Number of rainy days	Year 2 Rainfall (mm)	Year 3 Number of rainy days	Year 3 Rainfall (mm)	Year 4 Number of rainy days	Year 4 Rainfall (mm)	Year 5 Number of rainy days	Year 5 Rainfall (mm)	Year 6 Number of rainy days	Year 6 Rainfall (mm)	Year 7 Number of rainy days	Year 7 Rainfall (mm)
January	4	1.9	6	2.9	7	3.2	10	35.2	1	1.4	5	27.5	2	3.9
February	6	8.8	7	11.2	8	55.1	2	1.7	4	41.5	1	15.0	5	30.0
March	8	0.5	1	<0.1	10	14.3	4	0.6	2	9.4	5	88.9	2	13.9
April	4	0.4	3	4.0	7	10.4	3	20.6	1	1.0	1	2.4	—	—
May	—	—	2	<0.1	—	—	1	<0.1	1	0.2	1	3.8	—	—
June	—	—	—	—	—	—	—	—	—	—	2	22.0	1	0.1
July	—	—	—	—	1	<0.1	—	—	1	1.7	2	14.0	1	2.8
August	—	—	5	29.7	—	—	—	—	3	3.2	2	16.0	1	0.3
September	—	—	—	—	—	—	—	—	1	1.6	1	9.5	1	2.8
October	—	—	—	—	—	—	1	<0.1	1	0.1	5	54.2	1	0.1
November	—	—	—	—	—	—	1	<0.1	1	0.5	2	15.6	1	2.4
December	4	6.5	2	<0.1	4	7.2	1	<0.1	2	0.7	12	121.2	1	1.5
TOTAL	26	18.1	26	48.0	37	90.2	23	58.1	18	61.3	39	390.1	16	57.8

Drowning in a desert

Rainfall in desert areas is very unpredictable. Many months of drought may be followed by a torrential downpour. Careful study of 16.5 shows that, in August of year 2, five rainy days brought almost two-thirds of the year's rain. In a single day in February of year 6, 15 mm fell, while in the whole of year 1 only 18 mm were recorded.

When sudden storms do occur, river valleys which have been dry for months will fill rapidly, as shown in 16.6. People have even been drowned in these **flash floods**. The barren desert will then spring into life. 16.7 shows flowers growing between slabs of mud after rain.

▼ **16.6** Flash floods in Arizona

▼ **16.7** Vegetation after desert rain

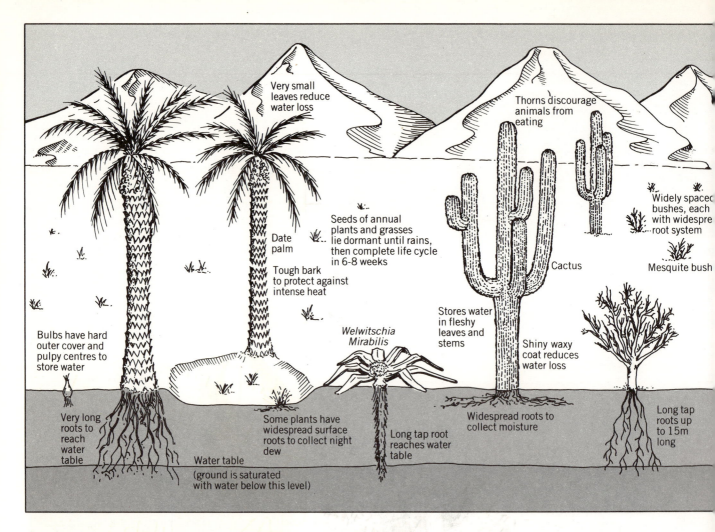

Very small leaves reduce water loss

Thorns discourage animals from eating

Date palm

Tough bark to protect against intense heat

Seeds of annual plants and grasses lie dormant until rains, then complete life cycle in 6-8 weeks

Widely spaced bushes, each with widespread root system

Cactus

Mesquite bush

Stores water in fleshy leaves and stems

Shiny waxy coat reduces water loss

Bulbs have hard outer cover and pulpy centres to store water

Welwitschia Mirabilis

Very long roots to reach water table

Some plants have widespread surface roots to collect night dew

Long tap root reaches water table

Widespread roots to collect moisture

Long tap roots up to 15m long

Water table (ground is saturated with water below this level)

Surviving the drought

Most parts of hot deserts have some plant life, and what seems to be a lifeless scene can be transformed by a heavy rainstorm into a mass of desert flowers and grasses. All desert plants have to be able to stand up to the high summer temperatures and last for long periods without rain. 16.8 shows some of the ways in which plants from different parts of the world are adapted to desert conditions. (The plants shown would not grow together naturally.) **Annual plants and grasses** complete their life cycle in a very short time, often in the cooler, and sometimes wetter, winter months. Their seeds then lie dormant on the ground, protected by thick cases, until the next rains. Other plants are adapted to live in a near-dormant state during the drought periods. Some have very long or widespread roots to reach

water stored in the ground. Others store water in their leaves and stems. Leaves are often small or needle-like, and outer cases or bark very tough, to reduce water loss.

▲ **16.8** Examples of desert vegetation from different parts of the world

▼ **16.9** Effects of irrigation on desert soil

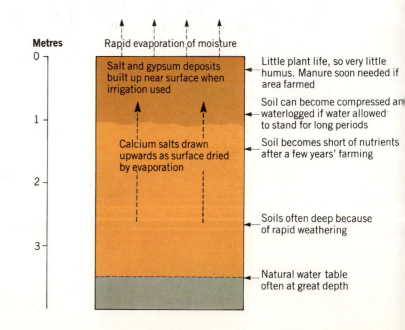

Metres

Rapid evaporation of moisture

Salt and gypsum deposits built up near surface when irrigation used

Little plant life, so very little humus. Manure soon needed if area farmed

Calcium salts drawn upwards as surface dried by evaporation

Soil can become compressed and waterlogged if water allowed to stand for long periods

Soil becomes short of nutrients after a few years' farming

Soils often deep because of rapid weathering

Natural water table often at great depth

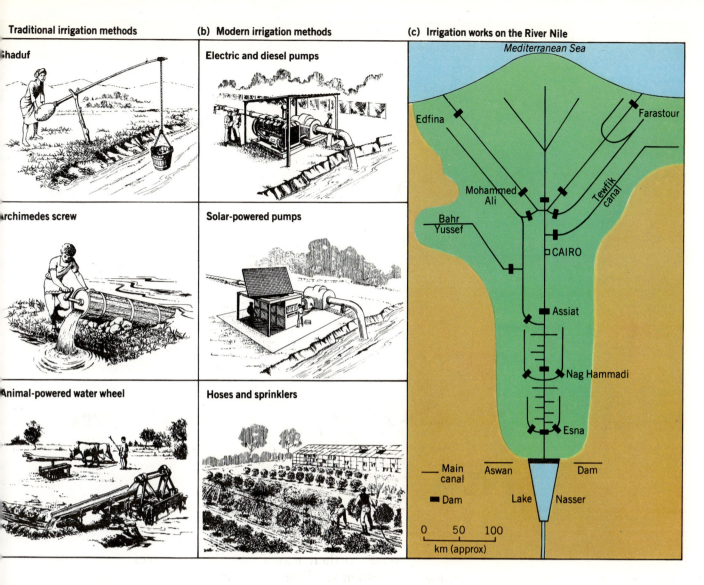

Traditional irrigation methods	(b) Modern irrigation methods	(c) Irrigation works on the River Nile
Shaduf	Electric and diesel pumps	
Archimedes screw	Solar-powered pumps	
Animal-powered water wheel	Hoses and sprinklers	

▲ 16.10 Irrigation

When **irrigation** water is supplied, some desert soils can make good farmland. 16.9 shows how the rapid **evaporation** of moisture draws calcium salts upwards, and for a few years the soil may seem quite fertile. However, the diagram also shows some of the problems irrigation can cause. Most serious is the build-up of salts on or near the surface. In Iraq 1% of the cultivated area is lost because of this each year. The soil may also become compressed and waterlogged if water is allowed to stand for long periods.

The lack of **humus** makes it important to add manure. In Israel human sewage has been used very successfully. This both helps the soil and gets rid of otherwise unwanted materials.

16.10a and b show some of the traditional and more modern irrigation techniques. All rely on a constant supply of water from wells or rivers. 16.10c shows the way in which the River Nile, a large river flowing through a desert area, has been used to supply irrigation water.

The future

To develop desert areas huge amounts of money are required. Much of the money has come from the discovery and sale of oil. Oil money is already paying for the **desalination** (removing the salts) of sea water, and for research into **solar power** in these very sunny areas. This could lead to great changes in the landscape.

◀ **17.1** Tourists on a Mediterranean beach

▼ **17.2** Tourism in Spain compared with the UK, Scandinavia and West Germany

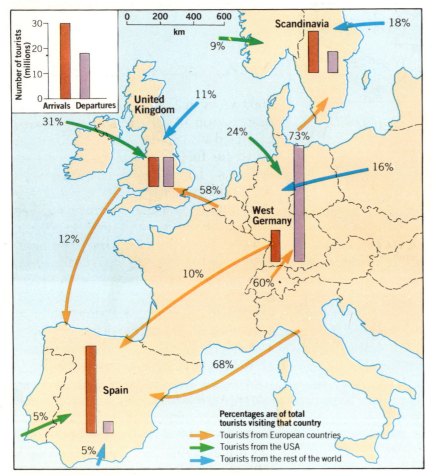

Percentages are of total tourists visiting that country
- Tourists from European countries
- Tourists from the USA
- Tourists from the rest of the world

◀ **17.4** Hours of sunshine per year

Copenhagen	1603	Alicante	3009
Edinburgh	1384	Athens	2756
Frankfurt	1563	Cadiz	3061
London	1514	Ibiza	2860
Warsaw	1676	Madrid	2843

Sunworshippers paradise

17.1 shows a scene typical of much o the Mediterranean coast from April t October. Mid-summer temperature are so high that people often leave th beaches in the middle of the day. Som tourists are attracted even in the coole months, since temperatures are sti much higher than in central and north ern Europe.

For countries such as Spain an Greece, the **climate** is one of the greatest advantages. Tourism is amon their most important industries. 17. shows the movement of tourists t Spain in a typical year, compared wit that to some cooler countries.

▼ **17.3** The climate of Athens

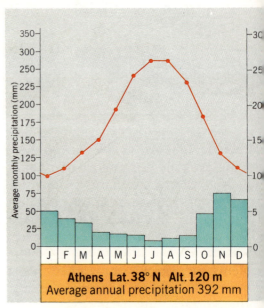

Athens Lat. 38° N Alt. 120 m
Average annual precipitation 392 mm

In 17.3 the hot dry summers an warm wet winters typical of Mediterra nean countries can clearly be seen Summers are dominated by the **sul tropical high pressure**, which mov northwards with the overhead sun fro the Sahara (see 12.4 and 12.5). In wint the sun's southward movement bring this area into the **temperate low pressure zone**, with wet wester

...winds and **frontal rain** (see page 51). In winter the Mediterranean Sea acts like a gigantic hot-water bottle, keeping coastal areas particularly warm. 17.4 shows how sunshine hours in Mediterannean resorts compare with other European locations. The other parts of the world which have a similar climate are shown in 17.5.

▶ **17.5** Areas of Mediterranean climate

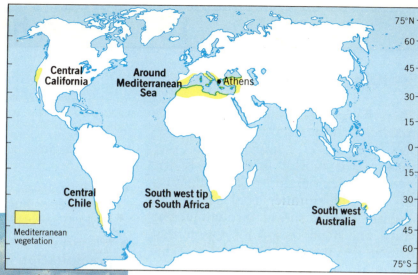

▲ **17.6** Woodland and scrub

◀ **17.7** Vines

◀ **17.8** Citrus fruits

Not-so-natural vegetation

2000 years ago a lot of the Mediterranean region had a **natural vegetation** of mixed woodland. Much has been cut down for fuel, building, or to clear the land for farms or settlements. 17.6 shows the typical vegetation today. It is a mixture of woodland shrubs and low scrubs. On sandy soils it is known as **maquis** but on drier limestone soils, where there are few trees and lower shrubs and scrub only, it is called **garrigue**. Removing the tree cover or overgrazing by animals such as goats has caused severe **soil erosion** in places. The original vegetation is seldom able to regrow once it has been cut down.

Most of the plants of this zone are **sclerophyllous**. This means that they can survive periods of drought because they have hard, leathery, thickened cuticles (outer skins) on their leaves. This is especially helpful in preventing the plant from wilting. Olive trees have such leaves, and also extremely deep roots, allowing them to gain water from below the levels which dry out. Most other native plants are adapted in a similar way, and some produce fruits which form a useful commercial crop. The olive and vine (see 17.7) are the best examples while citrus fruits (tangerines are shown in 17.8) have been introduced.

Sorting it out

The changeable nature of Britain's weather is often reported in the newspapers. However, compared with other areas of the world, Britain rarely has *extremes* of temperature or rainfall. Winters are mild, summers cool and rainfall is fairly evenly spread throughout the year. The main reason for this is that Britain is surrounded by water. This makes the **temperature range** much smaller than those found in the middle of a large landmass at similar latitudes (see·page 59). Winter temperatures are even higher because of the effect of a warm ocean current, the **North Atlantic Drift** (see 12.8, page 59). The winds blow most often from the west bringing rain from the Atlantic at all seasons.

18.1 shows the **climatic** variation within the British Isles. By looking carefully at the graphs certain patterns are seen:

● western areas are wetter than eastern areas;

● western areas have a winter rainfall maximum, but eastern areas have a more even distribution;

● hilly areas (e.g. Buxton) receive more **precipitation** because of **relief rainfall** (see page 50);

● western areas are cooler in summer and warmer in winter (have a lower temperature range) than eastern areas;

● the south east has the warmest summer temperatures and the greatest amount of sunshine throughout the year.

▼ **18.1** Climate difference in Britain

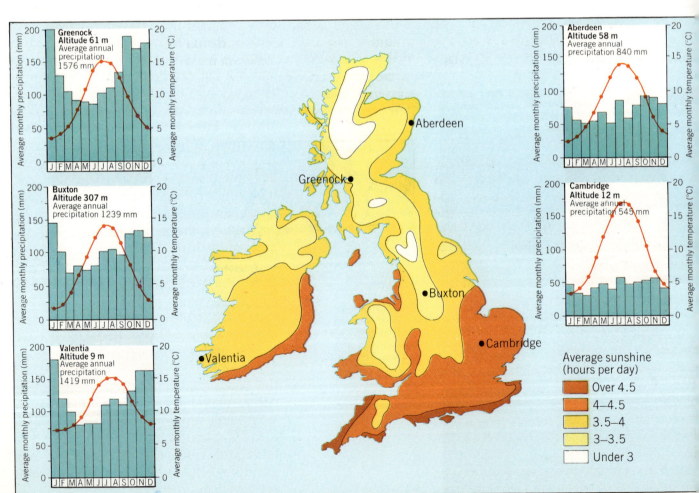

Polar maritime air (mP)

Source. North Atlantic, south of Greenland.

Character. Moist and cool with heavy showers from cumulus cloud. Good visibility. Affects us for 40% of the year.

Season. All year.

Arctic maritime air (mA)

Source. Frozen Arctic ocean and seas to south.

Character. Very cold and cloudy with heavy snow showers, especially in north and over hills.

Season. Winter.

Polar continental air (cP)

Source. Siberia and northern Scandinavia.

Character. Intensely cold and dry. Frosts and fogs may last all day. Some cloud and drizzle on east coast.

Season. Winter.

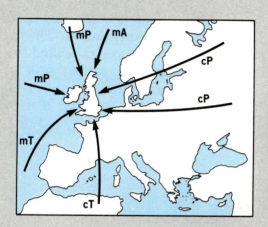

Tropical maritime air (mT)

Source. Tropical north Atlantic

Character. Moist and warm. May be clear or the cool sea around Britain may cause fog and low cloud. Thunderstorms common in summer.

Season. All year.

Tropical continental air (cT)

Source. North Africa

Character. Warm and very dry summer heatwaves. Unusually dry and warm weather, if arrives in other seasons.

Season. Mostly in summer.

The **maritime** effect is most marked in western areas. The **continental** mass of Europe has a greater influence on the climate of eastern Britain but the Atlantic's effect is still very strong.

Finding the source

Changes in weather are caused by the movement of air above the land. To explain the changeable nature of Britain's climate, we must look at the sources of the air that moves over Britain. 18.2 shows the five main areas from which Britain's weather comes. Each area gives the air above it (the **air mass**) certain characteristics. As the air mass moves over Britain it brings with it the characteristics from the source region. **Polar maritime air** and **tropical maritime air** are the most common. Some of the greatest sudden changes take place in winter when tropical maritime air replaces or is replaced by **polar** or **Arctic continental air**.

18.3 shows the paths of **depression** (see page 51) which bring rain from the

Atlantic. They are more frequent in winter giving the winter rainfall maximum in the west. **Convectional rainfall** (see page 50) is common in summer in tropical maritime air, especially in the eastern half of the country where temperatures are highest.

▲ **18.2** The air masses which affect Britain

▼ **18.3** Common depression tracks over Western Europe

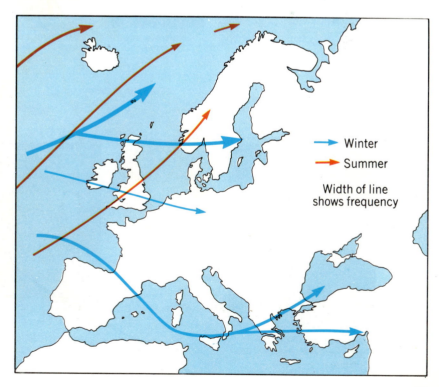

Winter

Summer

Width of line shows frequency

So much change

Very little **natural vegetation** is left in Britain. Hundreds of years of settlement, farming and industrial activity have removed the **hardwood trees** such as the oak which once covered much of the country. Even the remote peat-covered moorlands were once forested. But, after being cleared, the soils became waterlogged and trees would not grow again.

The effect of human action was the last in a series of changes in vegetation which have taken place in Britain since the end of the last Ice Age. 18.4 shows that, as temperatures rose, low-growing plants such as mosses began to cover the bare land. The area would have looked much like **tundra** regions do today (see 12.16, page 63). Then small trees established themselves, followed some 7500 years ago by **coniferous** forests, and finally by **deciduous** forests. (These trees were able to survive the cool winter months by shedding their leaves in autumn.) This change of vegetation through time is one example of a plant **succession**. The final stage of any succession is called the **climax vegetation**.

Clearing the forests for farming has changed the soil in Britain, as 18.5 shows. Originally a well-drained fertile

▼ **18.4** How the vegetation of Britain has changed

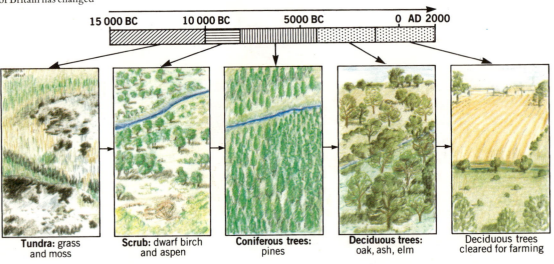

Tundra: grass and moss

Scrub: dwarf birch and aspen

Coniferous trees: pines

Deciduous trees: oak, ash, elm

Deciduous trees cleared for farming

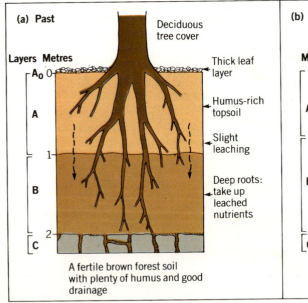

(a) Past

Deciduous tree cover

Layers Metres

A₀

Thick leaf layer

A

Humus-rich topsoil

Slight leaching

B

Deep roots: take up leached nutrients

C

A fertile brown forest soil with plenty of humus and good drainage

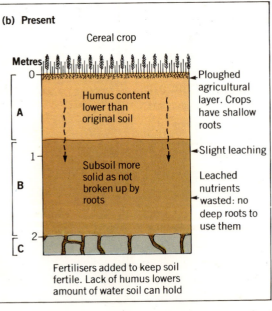

(b) Present

Cereal crop

Metres

Ploughed agricultural layer. Crops have shallow roots

A

Humus content lower than original soil

Slight leaching

B

Subsoil more solid as not broken up by roots

Leached nutrients wasted: no deep roots to use them

C

Fertilisers added to keep soil fertile. Lack of humus lowers amount of water soil can hold

◄ **18.5** Soils of eastern England, past and present

brown forest soil existed. Crops provide less **humus** and so soils become lighter in colour. Upland soils (over 200 metres) often become acidic because of peat formation, and have limited agricultural use. Drainage and using fertilisers are very costly. Some upland areas have been planted with coniferous trees which are adapted to the acid soils (see page 89). Other areas are left as open country important for recreation.

Extremes

As we have seen, Britain's climate is varied but extremes are uncommon. When they do occur their effects can be serious. Many of our homes and places of work are not designed for the very cold conditions occasionally found in winter (18.6a). Polar continental air from Siberia is usually the cause. Water pipes may freeze and heating systems cannot cope. Deaths from the cold (hyperthermia) rise rapidly. Unusually heavy snowfalls bring chaos causing roads and motorways to close. The huge cost of special equipment to clear a freak fall cannot be justified.

Because Britain normally has rain at all seasons, water is not stored in great quantities. When a severe summer drought occurs, therefore, the use of water has to be restricted by a ban on washing cars and watering gardens. Occasionally tropical continental air form North Africa brings very high summer temperatures (18.6b) welcomed by the holiday maker. The unusually hot weather also gives an enormous boost to the profits of ice cream, soft drinks and brewery companies.

18.7 shows clearly why the greatest concentration of seaside resorts in Britain is along the south coast. Places such as Bournemouth, Brighton and Margate are the sunniest and warmest areas of the country in July. There is severe overcrowding of roads leading to the coast and beaches on fine summer weekends.

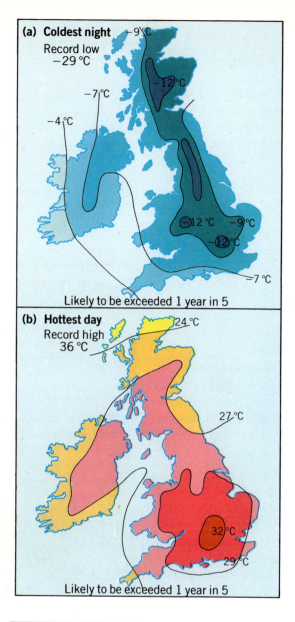

◄ 18.6 Extremes of temperature

(a) **Coldest night**
Record low −29 °C
−9 °C
−12 °C
−7 °C
−4 °C
−12 °C   −9 °C
−12 °C
−7 °C
Likely to be exceeded 1 year in 5

(b) **Hottest day**
Record high 36 °C
24 °C
27 °C
32 °C
29 °C
Likely to be exceeded 1 year in 5

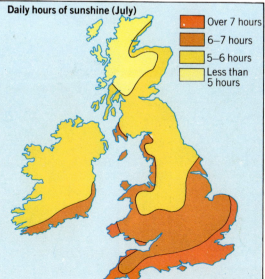

◄ 18.7 July sunshine in Britain

Daily hours of sunshine (July)
- Over 7 hours
- 6–7 hours
- 5–6 hours
- Less than 5 hours

19 Grassy plains

The effect of human activity on landscapes can be enormous. Few natural landscapes have been changed so rapidly and completely by people as the Prairies of North America. 19.1a shows the scene some 200 years ago, when the natural grassland and wildlife had changed very little for over 1000 years. 19.1b shows the Prairies today, when almost all the land is used for farming.

Great extremes

The **natural vegetation** of the Prairies was suited to the **climate**. In 19.2 the great **temperature range** typical of **continental** areas such as the Prairies can be seen. The summer is warm, but mid-winter is bitterly cold (−20 °C). In parts of the Russian Steppes, shown in 19.3, minimum temperatures below −60 °C are not uncommon. At Winnipeg, temperatures are below freezing point for five months of the year, and there are usually only about 100 days each year when farmers can be sure that there will be no frost.

Winters are dominated by high pressure and tend to be fairly dry, with powdery snow being blown around by

▲ **19.1a** The Prairies 200 years ago

◄ **19.1b** The Prairies today

◄ **19.2** The climate of Winnipeg

▼ **19.3** Areas of temperate grassland vegetation

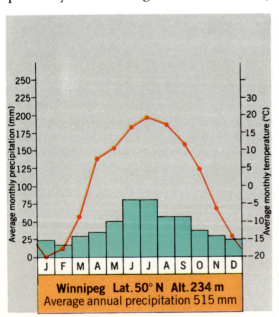

Winnipeg Lat. 50° N Alt. 234 m
Average annual precipitation 515 mm

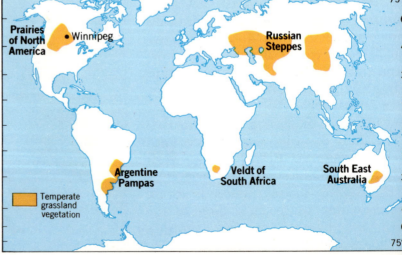

Prairies of North America
Winnipeg
Russian Steppes
Argentine Pampas
Veldt of South Africa
South East Australia

Temperate grassland vegetation

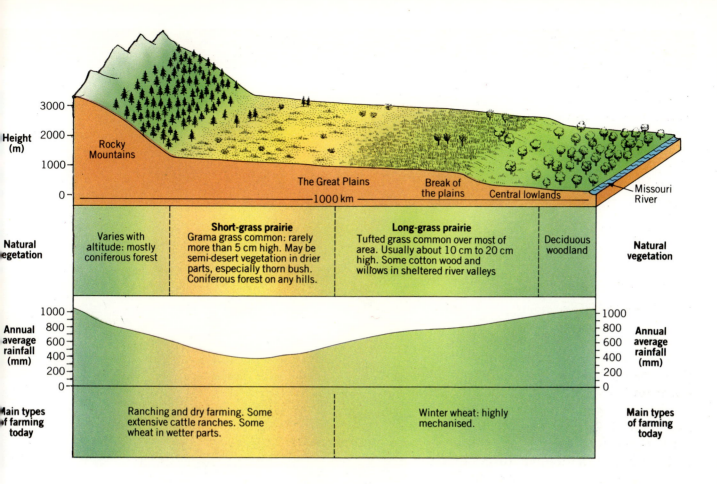

Height (m)	Rocky Mountains	The Great Plains	Break of the plains	Central lowlands	Missouri River

Natural vegetation

Varies with altitude: mostly coniferous forest	**Short-grass prairie** Grama grass common: rarely more than 5 cm high. May be semi-desert vegetation in drier parts, especially thorn bush. Coniferous forest on any hills.	**Long-grass prairie** Tufted grass common over most of area. Usually about 10 cm to 20 cm high. Some cotton wood and willows in sheltered river valleys	Deciduous woodland

Natural vegetation

Annual average rainfall (mm)

Annual average rainfall (mm)

Main types of farming today

Ranching and dry farming. Some extensive cattle ranches. Some wheat in wetter parts.	Winter wheat: highly mechanised.

Main types of farming today

fierce winds. In summer **convectional rain** is common, with thunderstorms often interrupting hot summer days.

Not-so-natural vegetation

19.4 shows the original vegetation of the Great Plains of North America, and the way in which annual rainfall was a major factor in deciding which plants would grow. Moving westwards from the Missouri River, rainfall declined, until trees could only grow along wetter river valleys. Long tufted grasses covered large areas. These *tall grasses* of the eastern Prairies eventually gave way to *short grasses* as rainfall declined. In some drier areas, thorn bushes and semi-desert plants were all that could survive.

However, there is little of this natural vegetation left today. Large numbers of settlers from Europe were encouraged by the American government to set up farms on the Prairies. The Indians and the natural wildlife were driven off, and European-style farms created.

The early success of these first settlers in the wetter Eastern Prairies encouraged others to push further west into the drier areas. A series of wetter than average years between 1898 and 1923 attracted even more. However, the rainfall of the western Prairies is very unreliable, and the 1930s brought years of drought. 19.5 outlines the disaster that followed.

▲ **19.4** The Great Plains: vegetation and rainfall

▼ **19.5** The American Dust Bowl

After 1862 the population of some parts of the Great Plains increased tenfold. The natural grasslands became deeply ploughed by farmers' efforts to increase grain harvests. The first grain production of the 1920s, coinciding with a rainy period, was so large that it earned the area the name of the 'Bread basket of America'. But by 1931 drought had taken these newly won cornfields into its relentless grip. Strong northerly winds began to shift the unprotected soils, lifting them into devastating dust storms. These were the fearful 'black dusters' which terrified the farmers and brought them to the verge of bankruptcy and starvation. In March 1935 a single storm blew for twenty-seven days and nights, when an eye witness described how 'it just rolled in from the north and you couldn't see your hand before your face at four in the afternoon.' Roofs fell in with the weight of the dust, while outbuildings became totally buried and roads disappeared.

Adapted from **John Whittow**, *Disasters* (Pelican)

Today the long-grass Prairie is one of the most productive farming areas in the world. In 19.6 the huge size and straight boundaries of the fields can clearly be seen. Huge machines do most of the work, with the result that few labourers are needed, and the area has a fairly low population density. The main crop is wheat, much of which is exported.

On the drier short-grass Prairies great care is now taken to prevent crop failure and **soil erosion** in dry years. In the driest areas cattle ranching (19.7) is common. Elsewhere, some crops are grown, but often fields are rested every other year, shelter belts are planted, and in hilly areas **contour ploughing** (see page 22) is used.

The rich black soil

Much of the success of Prairie farming has been due to the very fertile soils found in the area. In 19.8 the typical **chernozem soil** found over much of the Prairies is shown. The original grass cover had long roots. These produced **humus** deep in the soil when they died, making the soil dark and fertile often up to a depth of 1 metre. After being used for many years, however, the soil does now need fertilisers and manure added each year if it is to remain some of the richest farming land in the world. 19.8

▲ **19.6** Wheat growing in the Prairies

▼ **19.7** Ranching on the Prairies

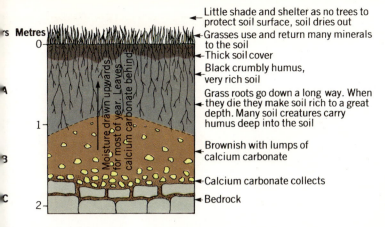

Little shade and shelter as no trees to protect soil surface, soil dries out

Grasses use and return many minerals to the soil

Thick soil cover

Black crumbly humus, very rich soil

Grass roots go down a long way. When they die they make soil rich to a great depth. Many soil creatures carry humus deep into the soil

Brownish with lumps of calcium carbonate

Calcium carbonate collects

Bedrock

Moisture drawn upwards for most of year. Leaves calcium carbonate behind

▲ **19.8** Chernozem soil

also shows that, with no tree cover, and now no grass cover, the sun and wind dry out the soil rapidly. This problem remains the most vital one for the Prairie farmer to solve.

Making it rain

Some scientists have tried to overcome the problems of dry years by making rain by a method called **cloud seeding**. By dropping dry-ice and silver iodide smoke from aircraft into cumulus clouds, it was hoped that the clouds would grow and eventually rain would fall.

In some places an increase of up to 20% in annual rainfall has been reported as a result of cloud seeding. But in other areas it has made no difference or is thought to have led to less rain. Much more research is needed before it will be the answer to the Prairie farmer's chief problem.

Weather hazards

Possible drought is not the farmer's only problem. In 19.9 two further hazards are shown, each of which could destroy the livelihood of any farmer in a few minutes.

▼ **19.9** Climatic hazards

(a)

Tornadoes are probably the most destructive weather hazard, for they can destroy everything in their path. The damage is caused by the very high winds (estimated at up to 800 km/h) and the very low pressure at the centre which makes buildings explode. The central spout is usually about 350 metres wide and travels at about 50 km/h. Tornadoes rarely last more than one hour, and on average travel about 25 km.

(b)

The huge hailstone which has dented the car in the photograph is large enough, but one 14 cm across and weighing 680 grams has been recorded in the Great Plains. One weighing 3.4 kg has been found in India. Large hailstones can completely flatten any crop, and the crop will not recover.

Hail may occur in any season but is usually formed in large thunderstorms in summer or autumn. Very strong convection currents whirl tiny ice particles up and down in a cloud. They keep on colliding, making bigger and bigger lumps of ice. Eventually they fall as hail.

20   Freezing cold

Areas which have low winter temperatures are shown in 20.1. Winter days are short and the sun is very low in the sky. Winter temperatures as low as −70 °C have been recorded in Siberia. Temperatures rise rapidly in the short summers because, although the sun is low in the sky, days are long.

These cold zones are affected by high pressure for most of the year and snow cover lasts for 6–8 months. Areas with a higher summer temperature are covered with **coniferous forest**. But the extreme north of North America and Eurasia, together with Antarctica, are too cold for tree growth because the ground remains permanently frozen below the surface. Low-growing **tundra vegetation** covers these areas. **Climate** details for forest and tundra areas are shown in 20.2a, b. The way the vegetation changes is shown by a **transect** across Siberia (20.3). The change from forest to tundra is gradual. At each point the vegetation is adapted to the climate.

▲ **20.1a** Coniferous forest

▲ **20.1b** Severe cold

▼ **20.1c** The cold lands

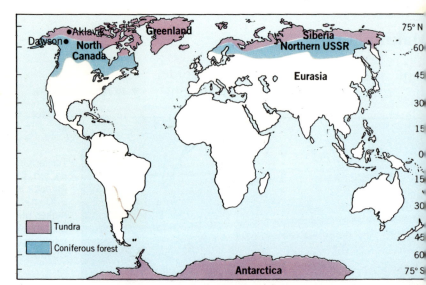

▼ **20.2a** Climate graph for coniferous forest region

◀ **20.2b** Climate graph for tundra region

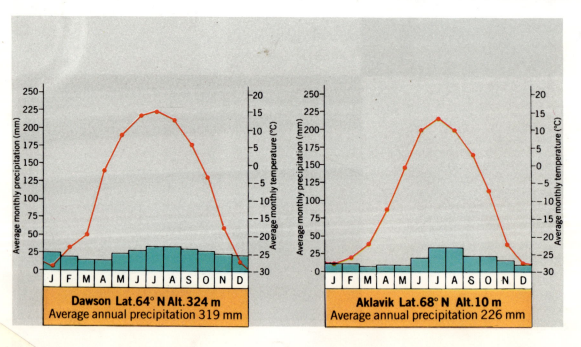

Dawson Lat. 64° N Alt. 324 m
Average annual precipitation 319 mm

Aklavik Lat. 68° N Alt. 10 m
Average annual precipitation 226 mm

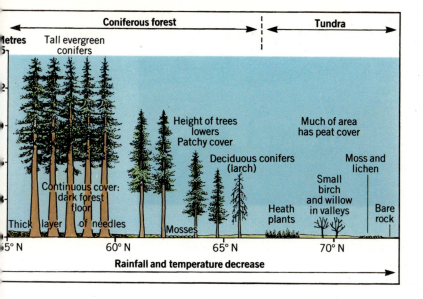

20.3 A transect along longitude 80°E: the west Siberian Plain

20.4 Tree growth rates in Sweden

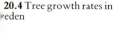

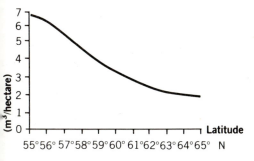

20.6 Podsol soil

The forests

Coniferous forest covers huge areas of land, almost unbroken. The **canopy** of the trees makes the needle-covered forest floor very dark, so little undergrowth can grow. Most of the trees are **evergreens** such as pine and spruce but in colder areas **deciduous** larch is common. Often one type of tree covers large areas (**pure stands**). The rate of tree growth falls as temperatures fall (20.4) and the place where winters become too long for tree growth is called the **tree line**. The ways in which coniferous trees are adapted are shown in 20.5.

The leaves	Other features
1. Evergreen leaves allow growth to begin as soon as temperatures are high enough. The growing season is very short.	1. Trees can live in very acid soils and need few minerals.
2. Needle-shaped leaves have a very small surface area, so water loss is very small: vital in dry winter winds.	2. Conical shape of tree, needle leaf shape and springy nature of branches all help to shed snow and prevent damage.
3. The thick skin of the leaf prevents wilting when water is not available.	3. Trees have a fan root system which is shallow. This allows growth to begin before the subsoil has thawed.
4. In very cold areas only the deciduous larch is found, which sheds its leaves to survive the coldest months. Evergreens cannot live as climate is too severe.	4. Larch trees are small and stunted in the very cold areas.
	5. Cones close up to protect seeds in harsh weather.

▲ **20.5** How coniferous trees are adapted to growing conditions

Acid soil

The typical soil in areas of coniferous forest is the **podsol** (20.6). The needles which fall to the forest floor take a long time to rot down, because of the low temperatures. A thick carpet of acidic rotted needles (peat) and fresh needles builds up. In spring, when the snow melts, the sudden release of water causes much **leaching** of iron and aluminium (20.6) down through the soil. These are often redeposited lower in the soil as a hard **ironpan** which may in time reduce drainage and cause waterlogging. The greatest danger of waterlogging is after tree clearance as the roots no longer help to break up the ironpan. Special machines can break up the pan but farmland (mainly pasture) still needs lime added each year to reduce acidity and encourage healthy plant growth.

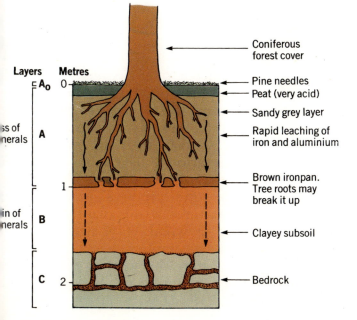

Tundra

20.7 shows the tundra in summer and winter. The main types of vegetation found were shown in 20.3. The only trees are stunted birches found in sheltered valleys. Much of the area is peat covered as the small amount of dead vegetation breaks down very very slowly. The surface is frozen for most of the year but in summer shallow lakes appear and much of the ground is marshy. Higher up, drier hillocks are covered with a vegetation mixture similar to British moorland (berried plants and heather). The characteristics of tundra vegetation are outlined in 20.8.

Soils are thin and permanently frozen below the top metre or so (20.9). The frost may go down to great depths. The summer thaw causes the surface layer to become waterlogged and to move slowly down slopes. Soil **horizons** (layers) are not found.

◀ **20.7a** Tundra in summer

◀ **20.7b** Tundra in winter

◀ **20.8** Characteristics of tundra vegetation

1. Lichens and mosses common in wetter areas. Berried plants (e.g. bilberries) common in drier areas. Stunted willow and birch found in some sheltered valleys.

2. The annual plants complete their life cycle in as little as 50–60 days. These plants germinate, grow, produce flowers and seed in the very short summer.

3. All plants are low growing, compact and rounded. They have no time to grow tall. The low growth protects them from wind.

4. Plants are shallow rooted and can survive waterlogged acid soil.

5. The plants are able to survive below the winter snow cover.

6. Apart from the brief flowering period, the tundra vegetation is drab.

▼ **20.9** Tundra permafrost soil

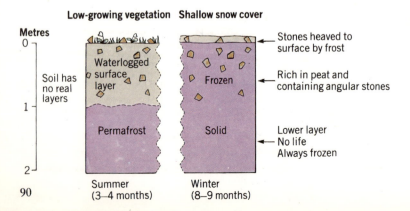

Using the timber

The pure stands of trees have been cut for **softwood** timber products for at least 50 years. The main felling season is winter when the sap content is at its lowest. Some trees are removed by road and rail but river floating to sawmills during the spring snow-melt is also important (20.10). The forests are not usually completely cleared but cut in strips so that seeds are available for **regeneration** in the cleared areas. New trees may also be planted. The demand for the forest products such as timber, manufactured boards (hardboard, chipboard, plywood, etc.), paper products and rayon continues to rise. A comparison of how the world's two greatest regions of forest are used is given in 20.11.

Wealth from the tundra

Native inhabitants of the few settlements on the tundra edges used to make a living by hunting and trapping fur-bearing animals and sea life. New settlers have been attracted to some areas by the discovery of valuable minerals such as oil. Icebreakers now keep sea access routes open during the short summer. The discovery of oil in North Alaska resulted in the building of a very long pipeline to exploit the oil wealth. However, the cold climate has created problems, as 20.12 shows.

20.10 Logging mill

20.11 A comparison of tropical and coniferous forest

20.12 The Trans-Alaskan pipeline

Tropical rain forest	Coniferous forest
Broad-leaved **evergreen hardwood** trees, e.g. teak, mahogany.	Needle-leaved **evergreen softwood** trees, e.g. spruce, pine.
Trees occur in **mixed stands**: makes exploitation difficult as many sorts of tree are mixed up. After felling, rapid growth of undergrowth causes extra problems.	Trees occur in **pure stands**: makes exploitation easy as all trees in one area are the same sort. No growth of undergrowth after felling.
Access often gained by rivers: timber floated to coast all year. Roads also built.	Access often gained by rivers: timber floated to coast in summer. Roads and rail links also built.
Found in developing countries. Forest products used in developed countries.	Found in developed countries. Forest products used in developed countries.
Labour supply may be available locally but is not skilled.	Labour supply usually not available locally. Skilled workers brought in.
Some areas poorly managed. Much of forest not replanted after clearance.	Forest well managed. Forest usually replanted as cleared.
Main use in hardwood furniture: very expensive.	Main use in buildings, paper and less-expensive furniture.

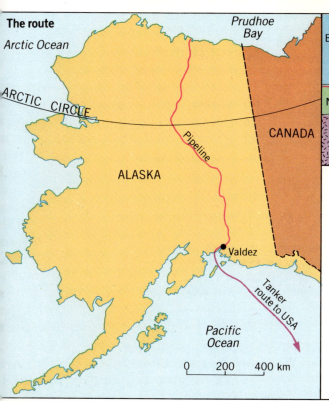

The route

Arctic Ocean

Prudhoe Bay

ARCTIC CIRCLE

Pipeline

CANADA

ALASKA

Valdez

Tanker route to USA

Pacific Ocean

0   200   400 km

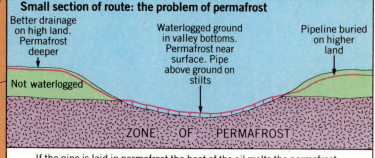

Small section of route: the problem of permafrost

Better drainage on high land. Permafrost deeper

Waterlogged ground in valley bottoms. Permafrost near surface. Pipe above ground on stilts

Pipeline buried on higher land

Not waterlogged

ZONE OF PERMAFROST

If the pipe is laid in permafrost the heat of the oil melts the permafrost and the pipe breaks as it sinks into the mud.

Key facts

1. Prudhoe Bay oil discovered 1968-9. Arctic Ocean is only ice free for a few weeks each year.
2. 1300 km pipeline planned to Valdez (ice-free port) where oil would be stored before tankers delivered it to the west coast of the USA. Pipeline can carry 600 000 barrels per day.
3. Permafrost caused major problems for pipeline engineers (see above diagram).
4. Conservationists objected to pipeline as it might interfere with the hundreds of thousands of caribou which migrate to tundra for summer grazing.
5. The delays and problems raised the cost of the pipeline from $1 billion to $4.5 billion.

Glossary

Terms have been explained here if they are important or if they were not described fully in the main text.

adaptations plant characteristics (e.g. leaf shape, flowering season) which plants have developed to make the most of the climate in which they grow naturally.

air mass a large (moving) body of air which has taken on the characteristics (temperature, pressure, etc.) of the area where it first formed (known as its source area).

altitude the height above sea level of a point on the earth's surface.

anticyclone an area where atmospheric pressure is higher than in the surrounding areas, usually bringing dry and calm weather.

aspect the compass direction in which a slope faces.

climate the average weather conditions of a place or region.

climax vegetation the type of vegetation which will eventually develop in an area if the climate remains the same for a long time.

condensation the change from a gas to a liquid, for example when steam (water vapour) cools and turns to water droplets (this is how clouds are formed).

coniferous (trees) cone-bearing trees with needle-shaped leaves which stay green throughout the year.

continental found in the interior of a large land mass (continent), far away from seas or oceans. A continental climate usually has colder winters, warmer summers and is drier than a maritime (coastal) climate.

convection current the movement caused by warm gas or liquid rising, and cold gas or liquid sinking.

convectional rainfall rain formed when warm moist air heated by the earth's surface rises and cools.

crust the outer layer of the earth. Continental crust is mostly granite and oceanic crust is mostly basalt.

cyclone a region of low atmospheric pressure usually bringing wet and windy weather.

debris a build-up of pieces of rock left by erosion or mass movement.

deciduous (trees) trees which lose their leaves at some season during the year.

deposition the laying down of material which has been moved by an agent of erosion, such as a river, glacier or the sea.

drainage basin the area of land that drains the rain water falling on it into one river system (which then carries the water to the sea, or a lake).

ecosystem the animals and plants living in a particular area and the way they are linked to it. As the animals, plants and environment are linked, any change in one will affect the others.

equatorial. within 10° latitude of the equator on the earth's surface. Equatorial climate type is only found on low ground in equatorial areas.

erosion the wearing away of the land surface by a variety of agents, the most important of which are the sea, rivers, glaciers and the wind.

evaporation the change from liquid to gas. Water on the earth's surface is evaporated by the sun's heat.

evergreen (trees) trees which do not lose their leaves at a particular season each year. Most, but not all, evergreen trees are coniferous.

extrusive (volcanic activity) volcanic activity which brings magma and other material to the earth's surface.

fault a break or fracture in the earth's crust along which movement has taken place.

flash flood a sudden flood of water caused by heavy rain which can be very dangerous when the water finds its way into narrow valleys.

freeze–thaw the weathering of rock due to repeated freezing and thawing of water within cracks in rocks.

front the line separating a warm air mass from a cold air mass at the earth's surface.

horizons layers found in soil, which can be seen if a pit is dug. The layers vary in colour and make-up, and tell us that soil has been forming at that place for a long time.

humus richest part of the soil made from decayed animals and plants. It is normally black and darkens the soil.

impermeable (rock, soil)   does not let water pass through.

intrusive (volcanic activity)   volcanic activity which brings magma into the crust below the earth's surface. This may come to the surface later if the rocks above are eroded.

irrigation   bringing water to areas of land to enable crops to grow in regions where rainfall alone would not be enough to keep them alive.

joints   cracks in rock which speed up the process of weathering.

leaching   the washing downwards of material such as humus and mineral salts in soil by rainwater.

lines of **latitude**   imaginary lines drawn around the earth, parallel to the equator, numbered in degrees north or south of the equator.

lines of **longitude**   imaginary lines running from the north to the south pole. 0° is the Greenwich meridian and 180° is the International Date Line. Lines in between are numbered in degrees east or west of the Greenwich meridian.

magma   molten (hot) material which is found below the earth's surface.

map projection   a way of drawing a part or the whole of the earth's surface on a flat piece of paper. Because the earth is round, it is not possible to do this with complete accuracy.

maritime   near to the sea or ocean. A maritime climate is influenced by nearness to the sea. It usually has cooler summers, milder winters and is wetter than a continental climate.

mass movement   the movement of weathered material downslope by gravity.

natural vegetation   the vegetation of a region before it has been changed by human activity.

outcrop   rock at the surface of the earth which is not covered with soil.

permeable (rocks, soil)   allows water to pass through.

plates   sections of the earth's crust which are moved over the earth's surface by convection currents.

polar (areas)   areas of the world around the north and south poles. These areas have very long cold winters and short cool summers.

precipitation   deposits of water, in any form, which reach the earth from the atmosphere, including rain, sleet, snow, hail, dew and frost.

range (temperature)   the difference between the highest and lowest temperatures in a given area over a fixed period of time (e.g. daily, monthly, yearly).

relief   the shape of the earth's surface: its valleys, mountains, plains, etc.

sediments   eroded materials carried downriver to the sea and deposited, often in great quantities.

soil   the loose material of the earth's surface in which plants grow.

soil erosion   the wearing away and loss of topsoil mainly due to wind, rain and running water.

soil profile   a cross-section through the soil which shows the different layers or horizons.

subsoil   the lower layer of the soil, often lacking in humus and containing a lot of weathered rock.

sub-tropical (areas)   areas of the earth's surface that are on the edges of tropical areas, at around 30°S and 30°N.

temperate (areas)   areas of the earth's surface roughly between 40° and 60° (north or south). These areas have a moderate temperature range during the year.

topsoil   the top layer of the soil, which is usually richer in humus than lower layers and more important for plant growth.

transect   a cross-section of an area of land, usually drawn to study changes in vegetation, land-use, relief, etc.

tropical (areas)   areas of the earth's surface between the Tropic of Cancer (23½° N) and the Tropic of Capricorn (23½° S).

tundra   a treeless low-lying region in the far north where the surface of the ground only thaws for a few weeks in summer. Below the surface, the ground is always frozen.

weather   the state of the atmosphere at a particular time including such things as atmospheric pressure, temperature, humidity, rainfall, cloudiness, wind speed and wind direction.

weathering   the ways in which rocks are weakened or broken down without being removed. The weathered debris may later be eroded.

Index